The
SmartCook
Collection

Chicken

LONDON, NEW YORK, MUNICH,
MELBOURNE, and DELHI

Senior Editor   Anja Schmidt
Art Director   Dirk Kaufman
Design Assistant   Erin Harney
DTP Coordinator   Kathy Farias
Production Manager   Ivor Parker
Executive Managing Editor   Sharon Lucas
Publisher   Carl Raymond

U.S. Recipe Adapter   Rick Rodgers

First published in 2003 by BBC Books
BBC Worldwide Limited
Woodlands, 80 Wood Lane
London W12 0TT

Published in the United States in 2005 by
DK Publishing, Inc.
375 Hudson Street,
New York, New York 10014

ISBN 0-7566-1924-6

Printed and bound in China by Toppan Printing
Co., (Shenzen) Ltd.
Color separation by Radstock Reproduction Ltd·
Midsomer Norton
Additional color work by Colourscan, Singapore

Cover and title-page photographs: Michael Paul
For further photographic credits, see page 135

Discover more at
www.dk.com

Introduction

When I look back over my years of cookbook writing, I have to admit that very often, decisions about what to do have sprung from what my own particular needs are. As a very busy person, who has to work, run a home, and cook, I felt it was extremely useful to have, for instance, summer recipes in one book – likewise winter and Christmas, giving easy access to those specific seasons.

This, my latest venture, has come about for similar reasons. Thirty-three years of recipe writing have produced literally thousands of recipes. So I now feel what would be really helpful is to create a kind of ordered library (so I don't have to rack my brains and wonder which book this or that recipe is in!). Thus, if I want to make a chicken recipe, I don't have to look through the chicken sections of various books, but have the whole lot in one convenient collection.

In compiling these collections, I have chosen what I think are the best and most popular recipes and, at the same time, have added some that are completely new. It is my hope that those who have not previously tried my recipes will now have smaller collections to sample, and that those dedicated followers will appreciate an ordered library to provide easy access and a reminder of what has gone before and may have been forgotten.

Delia Smith

Conversion Tables

All these are approximate conversions, which have either been rounded up or down. In a few recipes it has been necessary to modify them very slightly. Never mix metric and imperial measures in one recipe, stick to one system or the other.

All spoon measurements used throughout this book are level unless specified otherwise.

All butter is salted unless specified otherwise.

All recipes have been double-tested, using a standard convection oven.

Weights

½ oz	10 g
¾	20
1	25
1½	40
2	50
2½	60
3	75
4	110
4½	125
5	150
6	175
7	200
8	225
9	250
10	275
12	350
1 lb	450
1 lb 8 oz	700
2	900
3	1.35 kg

Volume

2 fl oz	55 ml
3	75
5 (¼ pint)	150
10 (½ pint)	275
1 pint	570
1¼	725
1¾	1 litre
2	1.2
2½	1.5
4	2.25

Dimensions

⅛ inch	3 mm
¼	5
½	1 cm
¾	2
1	2.5
1¼	3
1½	4
1¾	4.5
2	5
2½	6
3	7.5
3½	9
4	10
5	13
5¼	13.5
6	15
6½	16
7	18
7½	19
8	20
9	23
9½	24
10	25.5
11	28
12	30

Oven temperatures

Gas mark	°F	°C
1	275°F	140°C
2	300	150
3	325	170
4	350	180
5	375	190
6	400	200
7	425	220
8	450	230
9	475	240

Contents

Spring

Quick Roast Chicken with Lemon and Tarragon
Serves 4

1 (3-pound) chicken

2 tablespoons softened butter

2 ½ tablespoons chopped
fresh tarragon leaves

2 garlic cloves, crushed
through a press

Salt and freshly ground
black pepper to taste

1 lemon: ½ of it thinly sliced and
the slices halved, plus the juice of
the remaining ½ lemon

1 tablespoon olive oil

1 ¼ cups dry white wine

You will also need a 9- x 13-inch
flameproof roasting pan.

This is the best way to roast a small chicken. The flavorings can vary in any way you like – crushed chopped rosemary leaves, sage leaves, or thyme can be used, or a mixture of herbs, and you could replace the garlic with a couple of finely chopped shallots. It's a great recipe for adapting to whatever you have handy.

1. Begin by taking the chicken from the refrigerator about an hour before you intend to cook it (if it's a hot day give it about 30 minutes only). This will take the chill off the bird and help it to cook in the shorter time.

2. Preheat the oven to 450°F. Now make a garlic and herb butter by placing the butter, 2 tablespoons of the tarragon, and the garlic in a bowl and combine them with a fork, adding some salt and pepper. Then place the herb butter inside the body cavity of the bird, along with the halved lemon slices. Smear a little of the olive oil over the base of the roasting pan, place the chicken in it, then smear the rest of the olive oil all over the skin of the bird. Lastly, season well with salt and pepper. Place the roasting pan into the lower third of the oven. Now let it roast for 45 minutes without opening the oven door. When this time is up, remove the pan from the oven. Next, put a wooden spoon into the body cavity and, using a spatula to hold the breast end, tip the chicken and let all the buttery juices and slices of lemon pour out into the roasting pan. Transfer the bird to a carving board, cover with aluminum foil, and let it rest for 20 minutes

3. Meanwhile, using a tablespoon, skim off the excess fat from the juices in the roasting pan, then place the pan over high heat, add the wine and the juice from the lemon half and let it boil and reduce to about half its original volume. Now add the remaining ½ tablespoon tarragon, taste and check the seasoning. Carve the chicken and place on to warm plates and add any carving juices to the sauce. Spoon the sauce over the chicken and serve.

Chinese Chicken Thighs with Ginger and Star Anise
Serves 4

8 chicken thighs

⅔ cup Chinese rice wine or dry sherry

⅓ cup Japanese soy sauce

4 garlic cloves, crushed through a press

5 whole star anise

2 teaspoons grated fresh ginger

1 teaspoon Asian dark sesame oil

To garnish

1 red chili, deseeded and cut into fine shreds

1 scallion, white and green parts, cut into fine shreds

You will also need a wide flameproof casserole to hold the chicken, slightly overlapping, in a single layer.

The combination of ginger and star anise with a slick of sesame oil is irresistible. It's hard to believe something so easy can be both low in fat and taste so very good. Once you've tried this, it should become one of your family favorites. Serve the chunks of chicken on a bed of plain rice with a drizzle of the braising sauce, shreds of red pepper, and scallion for a colorful garnish.

1. First of all, remove the skin from the chicken, then place the thighs in the casserole. Now mix the rice wine, soy sauce, garlic, star anise, ginger, and sesame oil together in a bowl with ¼ cup of water and pour this mixture over the chicken, place the casserole over medium heat, and bring the liquid to a boil.

2. Meanwhile, preheat the oven to 400°F. Now transfer the casserole to the oven (no need to cover) and bake on the center rack for 40 minutes, turning the chicken halfway through the cooking time, until the chicken shows no sign of pink when pierced at the bone.

Garlic and Rosemary Chicken Brochettes with French Lentils
Serves 4

4 boneless chicken breasts, preferably with skin on (6 oz each)

1 medium red onion

Grated zest of 2 lemons, plus 6 tablespoons of fresh lemon juice

6 tablespoons extra virgin olive oil

8 shiitake mushrooms, stems removed

2 tablespoons fresh rosemary leaves, bruised and finely chopped

4 fresh bay leaves, snipped in half

2 garlic cloves, crushed through a press

Salt and freshly ground black pepper to taste

For the lentils

1 cup lentils, preferably French Puy lentils

1 small red onion

2 tablespoons extra virgin olive oil

2 cups hearty red or dry white wine or water

A large fresh rosemary sprig

Salt and freshly ground black pepper to taste

Fresh flat-leaf parsley to garnish

You will also need 4 (12-inch) wooden skewers, or use metal skewers.

Both the zest and its juice are used in this light marinade, fragrant with garlic and rosemary. Bay leaf, red onion, and mushrooms also add flavor as well as color to the skewered chicken, which can be marinated in the morning and grilled or broiled when you get home from work. While lentils are suggested as an accompaniment here, the brochettes could just as well be served with rice or potatoes.

1. Begin by cutting each chicken breast into 5 evenly sized pieces and place these in a bowl. Then cut one half of the onion into quarters and separate into layers, adding them to the chicken, along with the rest of the ingredients and a seasoning of salt and pepper. Now give everything a good mixing, cover, and leave it in a cool place for at least half an hour and up to 2 hours.

2. While you are marinating the chicken, if you are using wooden skewers you need to soak them for 30 minutes in hot water (to prevent them from burning). Next, see to the lentils. Just chop the other onion finely, heat the oil in a medium saucepan, cook the onion for about 5 minutes. Stir in the lentils, making sure they get a good coating of oil. Then add the wine and rosemary sprig. Put on the lid and let the lentils simmer gently for 40 minutes until the lentils are tender and the liquid has been absorbed. Then when you are ready to cook the chicken, preheat the broiler for 10 minutes on it highest setting and place the broiler rack 4 inches from the source of heat.

3. To cook the chicken, thread the pieces on the skewers, putting half a bay leaf first, then a mushroom, next a piece of chicken, then a piece of onion, finishing with the other mushroom and the other half of the bay leaf. Then, keeping the skin side of the chicken pieces upwards, lay the skewers on the grill rack, with a broiler pan underneath to catch the juices. Season them well with salt and pepper, then broil for 20 minutes, turning once and basting with the marinade juices once or twice. When the chicken is ready, taste and season the lentils with salt and pepper and arrange them on warm serving plates. Slide the food off the skewers between the prongs of a fork, then spoon the warm basting juices over everything. Garnish with flat-leaf parsley and a green salad.

Stir-Fried Chicken with Lime and Coconut Milk
Serves 4

4 boneless and skinless chicken breasts (6 oz each)

Grated zest and juice of 2 large limes

1 ½ tablespoons olive oil

2 green chilies, deseeded and finely chopped

1 ⅓ cups canned coconut milk

2 tablespoons Thai fish sauce

½ cup lightly packed fresh cilantro leaves

4 scallions, white and green parts, cut into 1-inch long shreds

Cooked jasmine rice, for serving

You will also need a very large skillet or a wok.

Thai flavors brighten this simple and quick supper dish. After marinating the chicken, preparation will take less time than you need to make the rice.

1. First of all, chop the chicken into bite-sized pieces and place them in a bowl with the lime juice and zest. Stir well, cover, and leave them to marinate in a cool place for as long as you have time, preferably 1 hour, but less is fine.

2. When you're ready to cook the chicken, heat the oil in the pan over high heat, add the chicken, and stir-fry for 3 to 4 minutes, until they're golden. Then add the chilies and stir-fry for 1 more minute. Add the coconut milk, fish sauce, and half the cilantro and scallions. Cook for another 1 to 2 minutes. Serve with Thai jasmine rice, with the remaining cilantro and scallions sprinkled on top.

White Chicken Chili with Pinto Beans and Fresh Tomato Salsa

Serves 6

30 fresh cilantro sprigs

2 tablespoons olive oil

2 large onions, sliced

2 jalapeño chilies, deseeded and finely chopped

4 garlic cloves, crushed

1½ teaspoons cumin seeds

1½ cups dried pinto beans, soaked overnight and drained

1 tablespoon all-purpose flour

2 cups hot chicken stock

1 teaspoon hot red pepper sauce

1 large green bell pepper

2¼ pounds boneless and skinless chicken thighs

Salt and freshly ground black pepper to taste

2 cups (8 oz) shredded Monterey jack cheese

⅓ cup heavy cream

Juice of ½ lime

For the salsa

9 ounces yellow or red tomatoes

Half the reserved cilantro leaves, roughly chopped

½ small red onion, finely chopped

Juice of ½ lime

A few drops of hot red pepper sauce

Salt and freshly ground black pepper to taste

You will also need a medium flameproof casserole with a lid.

This Southwestern stew uses Mexican ingredients in unconventional ways for a flavor-packed chili. Ideally, soak the beans overnight; alternatively, cover them with at least 2 inches of water, bring to a boil, boil for 10 minutes, then remove from the heat and let soak for 2 hours before draining and proceeding with the recipe. Serve with rice.

1. Begin by stripping the cilantro leaves into a small bowl, then cover the bowl with plastic wrap and reserve in the refrigerator. Now chop the cilantro stalks very finely. Next, heat the oil in the casserole and, over a gentle heat, cook the onions, chilies, garlic, and cilantro stalks for about 10 minutes, stirring once or twice until softened.

2. Meanwhile, dry-roast the cumin seeds in a frying pan for about a minute or until they become fragrant. Then grind the seeds to a powder in a pestle and mortar, then add them, along with the drained beans, to the casserole and stir. Now sprinkle in the flour and give it another good stir. Next, gradually add the stock, followed by the red pepper sauce, and a little salt. Bring everything to a simmer and cook, covered, on the lowest heat possible for 1¼ to 1½ hours, until the beans are tender.

3. In the meantime, make the salsa. First, skin, deseed, and finely chop the tomatoes. Then simply combine half the reserved cilantro leaves and the rest of the salsa ingredients and season. Mix well, cover, and leave aside to allow the flavors to develop.

4. After the chili has cooked, deseed the green pepper and cut it into ½-inch pieces. Cut the chicken into bite-sized chunks and stir them, along with the pepper, into the casserole, season well with salt and pepper, then cover, and simmer for 30 minutes.

5. In the meantime, mix the cheese with the heavy cream, then, when the 30 minutes are up, add it to the casserole. Simmer gently, uncovered, for another 20 to 25 minutes, stirring now and again, by which time the cheese will have melted into a smooth sauce. Finally, stir in the lime juice and the remaining cilantro leaves. Pass the salsa separately.

Poached Chicken Breasts with Morels in Cream Sauce

Serves 4

½ cup (½ oz) loosely packed dried morel or chanterelle mushrooms

2 cups dry white wine

4 chicken breasts with skin and bone (about 8 oz each)

Salt and freshly ground black pepper to taste

4 ounces cremini mushrooms, thinly sliced

4 large egg yolks

¼ cup heavy cream

2 tablespoons finely chopped fresh parsley

This has a wonderful, light creamy sauce. Morels have a mildly smoky flavor, but nutty chanterelles provide a fine alternative. Dried porcini, or cepes, can also be used, but they should be coarsely chopped after soaking.

1. Start by soaking the morels or chanterelles. Place them in a small bowl, cover with boiling water, and set aside to soak for 30 minutes. After that, strain them in a sieve and squeeze them to get rid of any surplus water. (You can reserve the soaking water, which can be frozen and is great for soups.)

2. Now preheat the oven to 150°F, ready to keep the chicken warm later. Next, in a large saucepan bring the wine to a simmer. Add the chicken breasts, together with some salt and pepper. Bring back to simmering, put the lid on, and simmer gently for 30 minutes, until the chicken looks opaque when pierced in the center. Then transfer the chicken to a heatproof plate, cover with aluminum foil, and warm in the oven.

3. Now boil the cooking liquid quite fast (without a lid) over high heat until it has reduced in volume by about half, adding the fresh and dried mushrooms towards the end of this time. Remove the pan from the heat. Next, in a small bowl, beat together the egg yolks and cream, mix a couple of tablespoons of the hot cooking liquid into the egg mixture, then pour the whole mixture back in to join the rest in the saucepan.

4. Return the pan to low heat and, stirring all the time, reheat it just until it thickens. Don't, whatever you do, let it come to the boil or it will separate! As soon as it has thickened, stir in the parsley. Pour the mushroom sauce over the chicken and serve with roasted butternut squash, if you wish.

Spiced Grilled Chicken with Green Couscous
Serves 4

For the marinade

2 garlic cloves

Salt, as needed

2 teaspoons grated fresh ginger

2 medium green chilies, deseeded

2 tablespoons fresh cilantro leaves

2 teaspoons ground turmeric

Freshly ground black pepper to taste

1 ½ cups buttermilk

For the chicken

4 boneless and skinless chicken breasts (6 oz each)

12 fresh bay leaves, cut in half

1 medium red onion, halved and separated into 16 layers

1 large yellow bell pepper, deseeded and cut into 16 equal pieces

Salt and freshly ground black pepper to taste

2 teaspoons peanut or other flavorless oil

For the couscous

2 cups (10 ounces) couscous

2 ¼ cups boiling chicken or vegetable stock

Salt and freshly ground black pepper to taste

4 scallions, white and green parts, finely chopped

¼ cup chopped fresh cilantro

½ cup finely chopped arugula

Fresh ginger and Indian spices combine with silky buttermilk for an oil-free (and low-fat) marinade that tenderizes the chicken while it enhances the flavor. Instant couscous is tossed with chopped scallions, cilantro, and pungent arugula to make a tasty and colorful bed for the chicken brochettes. Cilantro Chutney (page 62) makes a lively accompaniment.

1. First of all, you need to make the marinade. To do this, use a pestle and mortar to crush the garlic with about ½ teaspoon of salt until it becomes a purée. Next, add the grated fresh ginger. Then chop the chili and cilantro leaves and mix these with the garlic and ginger, along with the turmeric and some pepper. After that, pour the buttermilk into a bowl and whisk the other ingredients into it.

2. Now cut each chicken breast into 5 pieces, add them to the bowl, and give everything a good stir. Then press the chicken down well into the marinade, cover the surface with plastic wrap, and refrigerate for a few hours or, preferably, overnight. When you are almost ready to cook the chicken, if using wooden skewers, soak them in hot water for 30 minutes (to prevent them from burning). Preheat the broiler on its highest setting for at least 10 minutes and line the broiler pan with aluminum foil.

3. Next, dry the skewers in a clean tea cloth and thread half a bay leaf onto each one, then a piece of chicken, a piece of onion, and a piece of yellow pepper. Carry on alternating the bay leaf, chicken, onion, and pepper until you have threaded 5 pieces of chicken on to each skewer, finishing with half a bay leaf on each. Make sure you pack everything together as tightly as possible, then season with salt and freshly ground black pepper and brush the vegetables with a minute amount of oil. Lay the brochettes on the broiler rack and place them about 4 inches from the heat source. Brush liberally with some of the remaining marinade and grill them for 10 minutes. Turn them over, brush with the remaining marinade, and grill them for a further 10 minutes until they are cooked through, watching them carefully so they don't burn.

4. While the chicken is cooking, place the couscous in a large bowl, then pour the boiling stock over it. Add some salt and pepper and stir it with a fork. Then set aside

2 limes cut into wedges, for serving

You will also need 4 (10-inch) wooden skewers or use metal skewers.

for 5 minutes, by which time it will have absorbed all the stock and softened. After that, fluff it up by making cutting movements across and through it with a knife. Then stir in the remaining couscous ingredients and season to taste. When the chicken is ready, place the brochettes on top of the couscous and serve immediately on warmed dinner plates with the lime wedges.

Creamed Chicken with Avocado
Serves 4

4 tablespoons butter

⅓ cup all-purpose flour

1¼ cups milk

⅔ cup chicken stock

⅔ cup half-and half or light cream

1 (2.2-pound) store-bought, cooked chicken, cut into small strips (about 3 cups)

1 tablespoon dry sherry

Salt and freshly ground black pepper to taste

2 or 3 teaspoons fresh lemon juice, plus more for sprinkling

2 ripe avocados

¼ cup shredded Gruyère cheese

You will also need an 8-inch square baking dish.

Here's an original way to use a rotisserie chicken for a simple family supper you can throw together in a flash. Serve with wild rice and glazed carrots.

1. Preheat the oven to 400°F. Begin by melting the butter in a medium saucepan over low heat, add the flour, and blend to a smooth paste. Cook for 2 minutes, then gradually stir in the milk, stock, and half-and-half and, stirring all the time, bring it to a simmer and cook very gently for 2 or 3 minutes. Then remove the pan from the heat, add the chicken, sherry, and the salt, pepper, and lemon juice to taste, and stir everything together until combined.

2. Now halve and quarter the avocados and, having removed the stone and skins, slice the flesh thinly and cover the base of the dish with the slices. Sprinkle over a little lemon juice, spoon the chicken mixture on top and, finally, add the grated cheese. Transfer to the oven and bake from 20 to 25 minutes or until the sides begin to bubble.

Herb-Marinated Chicken Kebabs
Serves 2

2 boneless chicken breasts, preferably with skin (6 oz each)

½ medium red onion

½ yellow bell pepper, deseeded

1½ teaspoons chopped fresh thyme leaves

1½ teaspoons chopped fresh rosemary

2 bay leaves

2 lemon slices, cut in half

10 whole black peppercorns

2 garlic cloves

¼ cup white wine vinegar or cider vinegar

¼ cup extra virgin olive oil

Salt and freshly ground black pepper to taste

You will also need a 1-quart jar, plus 2 (10- to 12-inch) bamboo skewers, or use metal skewers.

A sprightly vinaigrette enlivened with lemon, garlic, and herbs prepares chicken for a perfect grill. Serve with grilled or steamed corn, broccoli, and sliced ripe tomatoes.

1. Begin by cutting each chicken breast into 5 pieces and placing them in the jar. Then cut the onion into 2 quarters and separate the layers (you'll need 8). Now cut the yellow pepper into 8 pieces and add these to the jar, along with the thyme and rosemary, bay leaves, lemon slices, and peppercorns. Now crush a clove of garlic and add this, too, plus the other clove, cut in half. Next, pour in the vinegar, followed by the oil, put the lid on the jar and give it a really good shake. Refrigerate overnight and give it another good shake in the morning.

2. Before cooking the chicken, if you are using wooden skewers you need to soak them for 30 minutes in hot water (to prevent them from burning). Preheat the broiler to its highest setting for 10 minutes. Then thread a bay leaf on to each skewer, followed by a lemon slice. Then alternate the chicken pieces with pepper and onion, finishing up with half a clove of garlic and the other slice of lemon. Add a seasoning of salt and pepper, then lay the skewers on the broiler rack, skin side up, with the broiler pan below to catch the juices. Position them about 4 inches from the source of the heat, then broil – turning once and brushing frequently with the marinade (do not baste during the last 5 minutes of broiling) – for 20 minutes, or until they are opaque when pierced with the tip of a knife. These are very nice served with rice and a mixed lettuce and arugula salad.

Chicken Paprikash
Serves 4

2 to 3 tablespoons peanut or other flavorless oil

4 chicken breasts with skin and bone (about 8 oz each) or 8 thighs

Salt and freshly ground black pepper to taste

2 medium onions, chopped

1 pound tomatoes, or 1 (14-oz) can plum tomatoes in juice, chopped

4 teaspoons hot Hungarian paprika, plus a little extra, for garnish

1 tablespoon all-purpose flour

2 good pinches of cayenne pepper

⅔ cup chicken stock

1 medium green or red bell pepper, deseeded and cut into small strips

⅔ cup sour cream

You will also need a large, deep skillet or a medium flameproof casserole with a lid.

This is nice served with some well-buttered noodles or some nutty brown basmati rice and a crisp green salad with a sharp, lemony dressing, or instead, serve with green tagliatelle tossed in butter with a sprinkle of poppy seeds.

1. Preheat the oven to 325°F. Begin by heating 2 tablespoons of the oil in the skillet and gently frying the chicken to a golden color; you will probably need to do this in two batches. As the chicken is ready, use a slotted spoon to transfer it to a plate, and season it with salt and pepper. In the remaining oil (add a little more if you need to), fry the onions gently for about 10 minutes to soften. Meanwhile, if you are using fresh tomatoes, skin them. To do this, pour boiling water over them and leave them for exactly 1 minute or 15-30 seconds if the tomatoes are small, before draining and slipping off their skins (protect your hands with a cloth if they are too hot). Then chop them.

2. Now stir the paprika, flour, and cayenne into the onions, with a wooden spoon, to soak up the juices before adding the chopped tomatoes. Stir them around a bit, then add the stock. Bring everything to a simmer, then return the chicken to the pan. Put the lid on and bake in the oven for 45 minutes. After that, stir in the chopped pepper, replace the lid, and cook for another 30 minutes.

3. Just before serving, spoon the sour cream all over, mixing it in just to give a marbled effect, then sprinkle on a little more paprika.

Spanish Chicken with Beans, Chorizo, and Tomatoes
Serves 4

1 ½ cups dried white kidney (cannellini) beans, soaked overnight and drained

A few sprigs of fresh thyme

2 bay leaves

2 tablespoons olive oil

1 medium onion

2 medium carrots

1 medium leek

2 celery ribs

2 tablespoons olive oil

4 chicken breasts, with skin and bone (about 8 oz each)

6 ounces smoked chorizo sausage

1 teaspoon sweet pimentón de la Vera (smoked paprika)

1 (14-oz) can chopped tomatoes

3 garlic cloves, chopped

A good pinch of saffron stamens

1 ¼ cups hot vegetable or chicken stock

Salt and freshly ground black pepper to taste

2 tablespoons chopped fresh parsley

You will also need a medium flameproof casserole with a lid.

Spanish smoked paprika, or *pimenton de la Vera,* is the secret ingredient in this recipe, and it's well worth searching out. You'll find it in the Spanish food section of many supermarkets, or it can be purchased online from any number of specialty food sites. Serve with plenty of crusty bread to mop up the tasty juices and a chicory-arugula salad.

1. Begin by cooking the beans. Place the soaked and drained beans in a pan with the thyme sprigs and 1 bay leaf and cover with water. Bring to a simmer, cover with a lid, and simmer the beans for 45 minutes to 1 hour or until the beans are tender. Meanwhile, prepare the vegetables. Begin by peeling the onion and carrots and finely chopping them. Next, take the tough green tops off the leek, then make a vertical split halfway down the center, and run it under cold water to rid it of any hidden grit. Then slice the leek in half lengthways and finely chop that too, followed by the celery ribs.

2. Next, heat 1 tablespoon of the olive oil in the casserole and when the oil is hot, brown the chicken breasts on both sides until golden. Then transfer the chicken to a plate and now add the rest of the oil to the casserole. Stir in the onions, carrots, leek, and celery and cook everything over a low heat, covered with the lid, to allow the vegetables to sweat in their own juices for 10 to 15 minutes or until they are beginning to soften.

3. While that is happening, you can prepare the chorizo sausage by peeling the skin off and dicing the sausage before stirring it into the vegetables with the paprika. Turn the heat up to medium and cook everything together for 2 to 3 minutes to draw the fat from the chorizo – you will need to stir constantly to prevent the chorizo from sticking to the bottom of the casserole. Now add the cooked, drained beans (you can throw away the thyme and bay leaf), tomatoes, garlic, the other bay leaf, and the saffron, followed by the hot stock. Season with salt and freshly ground black pepper and give everything a good stir. Place the chicken breasts on top, bring the whole lot to a simmering point, then reduce the heat to low and leave to simmer, covered, about 25 minutes, until they look opaque when pierced with the tip of a knife. Finally, transfer the chicken to warmed plates, and stir the parsley into the sauce before spooning it over the chicken.

Thai Red Curry Chicken
Serves 8

For the curry paste

4 medium red chilies, deseeded

Juice and zest of a lime

1 tablespoon finely chopped
lemongrass, tender part only

1-inch cube of fresh ginger

4 garlic cloves, peeled

4 shallots, peeled

1 teaspoon shrimp paste

2 tablespoons Thai fish sauce

For the chicken

8 chicken breasts with skin and
bone (7 to 8 oz each)

Salt to taste

1 tablespoon peanut or other
flavorless oil

To garnish

A few sprigs of fresh cilantro

2 limes, cut into quarters

This pungent curry paste is speedy to make and freezes well. So, you can make it in bulk, freeze and use it as and when you need it. This means you don't have to shop for small amounts of the ingredients. If you're really short of time, you can use ready-made bought Thai red curry paste.

1. To make the curry paste, all you do is put everything into a food processor or blender, and blend until you have a rather coarse, rough-looking paste. Remove the paste and keep it covered in the refrigerator until you need it. About 1 or 2 hours before you need to cook the chicken, lay the breasts in a medium baking dish, then take a sharp knife and make four diagonal cuts across each breast. Sprinkle first with a little salt and then with the oil, rubbing the oil well into the chicken. Next, spread the curry paste over the surface of each portion and rub that in well too. Cover with plastic wrap, and set aside in a cool place for the chicken to soak up all the flavors for 1 to 2 hours.

2. To cook the chicken, preheat the oven to 350°F. Remove the plastic wrap, then place the dish on a high rack and cook for 35 to 40 minutes, basting with the juices from time to time. Serve the chicken with rice, garnishing with sprigs of cilantro and some lime quarters to squeeze over.

Baked Curried Chicken Breasts
Serves 4

1 teaspoon salt

1 large garlic clove

1 ¼ teaspoons ground ginger

1 ¼ teaspoons ground turmeric

2 tablespoons peanut or other
flavorless oil

1 medium onion, chopped

4 chicken breasts with skin
and bone (8 oz each)

1 cup plain lowfat yogurt

4 teaspoons Madras-style
curry powder

1 teaspoon cornstarch

You will also need a medium
roasting pan.

This pungent curry paste is easy to make and freezes well. If you're really short of time, you can use ready-made Thai red curry paste. Serve with rice and buttered green beans.

1. Preheat the oven to 350°F. Begin by placing the salt in a mortar and crush it quite coarsely, then add the garlic and, as you begin to crush it and it comes into contact with the salt, it will break down into a purée. Next, add the ground ginger and turmeric, then the oil, and using circular movements, really work all the ingredients together until you have a thick brown paste.

2. Next, scatter the onion in a medium pan large enough to hold the chicken, and then, holding one of the chicken breasts in your hand and using a spatula, smear a quarter of the paste over both sides of the chicken breast and then place it on top of the onion before doing exactly the same with the other breasts. Now transfer the pan to the oven and cook the chicken on the middle rack for 30 minutes.

3. Meanwhile, in a bowl, whisk together the yogurt, curry powder, and cornstarch. Then, when the chicken has had its cooking time, spoon the yogurt over the chicken and cover the pan with aluminum foil before returning it to the oven for a another 30 minutes.

Summer

Chicken Salad with Tarragon and Green Grapes
Serves 4-6

One (3-pound) cooked chicken (use 1 ½ store-bought, rotisserie chickens, if you wish)

Salt and freshly ground black pepper to taste

⅔ cup mayonnaise

⅓ cup heavy cream

3 scallions, white and green parts, finely chopped

1 ½ teaspoons chopped fresh tarragon

1 small head romaine lettuce, washed and patted dry

1 cup seedless green grapes, halved

A few sprigs of watercress, for garnish

This is an old-fashioned chicken salad that still tastes fresh. It's one of the nicest cool dishes you can serve on a hot summer day. To dramatically cut the preparation time for this salad, use store-bought rotisserie birds.

1. First of all, remove the skin from the chicken and slice the flesh into longish pieces, where possible. Then, remove all the chicken from the bones. You should have about 4½ cups chicken. Place the meat in a large bowl, seasoning with salt and pepper.

2. Next, in a separate bowl, mix the mayonnaise thoroughly with the cream, adding the scallions and tarragon. Now pour the dressing over the chicken, mix it well so that all the chicken gets a good coating. Then arrange it on a plate of crisp lettuce leaves, scatter with the grapes, and garnish with a few sprigs of watercress.

Herbed Chicken Tartlets
Makes 6

For the filling

1 or 2 boneless and skinless chicken breasts (about 7 oz total)

¼ teaspoon ground mace

Salt and freshly ground black pepper to taste

5 ounces bulk pork sausage (I often use skinned pork sausages)

2 scallions, white and green parts, finely chopped

1 tablespoon chopped fresh parsley

1 teaspoon chopped fresh sage

½ teaspoon chopped fresh thyme, plus 6 small sprigs

1 teaspoon lemon juice and ½ teaspoon finely grated zest

1 tablespoon heavy cream

For the pastry

2 tablespoons milk

½ cup vegetable shortening

1⅔ cups unbleached flour, plus a little extra for rolling out the dough

½ teaspoon each dry mustard powder, dried thyme, and salt

A good grating of nutmeg

3 large egg yolks (2 yolks to be used for glazing the pies)

You will also need a muffin pan, preferably nonstick, with six cups (each one 3 inches across the top and about 1¼ inches deep), lightly

Individual double-crust pies, filled with boneless chicken encased in homemade sausage, are easy to form and bake in muffin tins. They're perfect for food on the move. Take along pickles, radishes, and mustard or mango chutney.

1. You need to start by making the filling. So, first of all, cut the chicken into ½-inch pieces, then place them in a bowl, add the mace and season with salt and pepper. Now, in a separate bowl, combine the sausage with the scallions, parsley, sage, thyme, lemon juice and zest. Add the cream and mix everything together well.

2. Preheat the oven to 350°F. Now for the pastry, put the milk and ¼ cup water into a small saucepan and add the shortening, cut up into small pieces. Place the pan over low heat and simmer until the fat has dissolved. Sift the flour, mustard, thyme, salt, and nutmeg into a large mixing bowl, and mix in 1 of the egg yolks so that it is evenly distributed.

3. When the fat has completely melted in the liquid, turn up the heat to bring just to a boil. Pour it on the dry ingredients and, using a wooden spoon, mix everything together. Then turn the dough out onto a lightly floured work surface and bring it together with your hands to make a ball. You have to work quickly now, as it's important that the pies go into the pan while this dough is still warm. Take two-thirds of the dough and cut this up into 6 equal parts. Roll each of these into a ball and put 1 into each of the holes in the pan. Using your thumb, quickly press each ball flat on to the base and then up to the top edge. Press the dough again so it extends about ¼ inch over the edge of the rim.

4. Using a teaspoon, divide half of the sausage mixture among the 6 pies. Then follow this with the chicken and then the rest of the sausage mixture, pressing the filling in firmly as you go. Then roll out the remaining dough on a work floured surface and cut out six 3-inch rounds; the dough will be quite thin, so you may use a little extra flour. Next, using a fork, lightly beat the remaining 2 egg yolks together in a small bowl. Then, using a pastry brush, paint some of the egg yolk round the upper edge of the pies and gently press on the lids. Using a small fork, press the rim of each lid against the top

of the pie case. Make a hole in the top of each pie and glaze with more yolk. Finally, push a small sprig of thyme into the top of each pie.

5. Now place the muffin pan on the baking sheet and bake the pies for 30 minutes on the center rack until the crust is lightly browned and set. After this time, using a thick cloth, carefully remove the hot pies from the pan and place them directly onto the hot baking sheet, a small round-ended knife is useful for getting the pies out of the pan. Glaze the sides of the pies with the remaining egg yolk and return them to the oven for 20 minutes more or until the sides and base of the pies are crispy. Cool on a wire rack. When cold, refrigerate in an airtight container; they'll keep like this for a couple of days, but bring them to room temperature before eating.

Basque Chicken and Rice with Chorizo, Olives, and Sun-Dried Tomatoes
Serves 4

1 (3½ pound) chicken, cut into 8 pieces

Salt and freshly ground black pepper to taste

2 large red peppers

1 very large or 2 medium onions

½ cup sun-dried tomatoes in oil

2 to 3 tablespoons extra virgin olive oil

5 ounces smoked chorizo sausage, skinned and cut into ½ inch–thick slices

2 large cloves garlic, chopped

1 cup brown basmati rice

1¼ cups chicken stock

¾ cup dry white wine

1 tablespoon tomato paste

½ teaspoon paprika, preferably Spanish hot paprika

1 teaspoon chopped fresh herbs, such as oregano and basil

½ cup pitted black olives, halved

½ large orange, peeled and cut into wedges

You will also need a wide, shallow, flameproof casserole with a domed lid, measuring about 9½ inches at the base.

The delicious combination of chicken and rice, olives, and peppers is typical of all the regions around the western Mediterranean but this Spanish version, with the addition of spicy chorizo sausage and a hint of paprika, is the best. The use of sun-dried tomatoes preserved in oil gives it even more character. This recipe will provide a complete supper for four from the same pot – it needs nothing to accompany it!

1. Start by seasoning the chicken pieces well with salt and pepper. Next, slice the red peppers in half and remove the seeds and pith, then slice each half into 6 strips. Likewise, peel the onion and slice into strips of approximately the same size. The sun-dried tomatoes should be drained, wiped dry with paper towels, and then cut into ½-inch pieces.

2. Now heat 2 tablespoons of olive oil in the casserole and, when it is fairly hot, add the chicken pieces – 2 or 3 at a time – and brown them to a nutty golden color on both sides. As they brown, transfer them with a draining spoon to a plate lined with paper towels. Next, add a little more oil to the casserole, with the heat slightly higher than medium. As soon as the oil is hot, add the onion and peppers and allow them to brown a little at the edges, moving them around from time to time, for about 5 minutes. After that, add the chorizo, sun-dried tomatoes, and garlic. Stir these around for a minute or two until the garlic is pale golden and the chorizo has taken on some color. Next, stir in the rice and, when the grains have a good coating of oil, add the stock, wine, tomato paste, and paprika. As soon as everything has come to a simmer, turn the heat down to a gentle simmer. Add a little more seasoning, then place the chicken gently on top of everything (it's important to keep the rice down in the liquid). Sprinkle the herbs over the chicken pieces and scatter the olives and wedges of orange in among them.

3. Cover with a tight-fitting lid and cook over the gentlest possible heat for about 50 minutes to 1 hour or until the rice is cooked but still retains a little bite. Alternatively, cook in a preheated oven at 350°F for 1 hour.

Barbecued Chicken Drumsticks with an Apricot Glaze
Serves 6

For the apricot barbecue glaze

2 large fresh apricots

3 tablespoons dark brown sugar

¼ cup Worcestershire sauce

¼ cup soy sauce

1 tablespoon grated fresh ginger

1½ teaspoons ground ginger

A few drops of hot red pepper sauce

2 tablespoons tomato paste

1 garlic clove

Freshly ground black pepper to taste

For the chicken

18 chicken drumsticks

½ cup dry white wine, optional

Since a sweet glaze burns easily, these drumsticks are sensibly cooked first in the oven, then brushed with the apricot glaze and finished on the grill. Serve with mashed potatoes, sautéed kale, and a spicy red wine, such as Zinfandel.

1. Begin by placing the fresh apricots in a small saucepan with enough water to cover them, then bring them up to simmering point and simmer for 2 minutes. Now drain off the water and, as soon as they are cool enough to handle, slip off the skins (protect your hands with a cloth if they're too hot). Then halve and stone them. Place the apricots in a blender or food processor, together with all the other glaze ingredients. Process everything to a purée and the sauce is ready. All you do now is arrange the drumsticks in a shallow dish, pour the glaze over them – turning the pieces of chicken so that each one gets a good coating – then cover and leave in a cool place until you're ready to cook, up to 2 hours.

2. Preheat the oven to 350°F. When you light your outdoor grill, bake the chicken drumsticks for 30 minutes. When the grill is hot, brush the drumsticks with the glaze and grill for about 5 minutes on each side about 3 inches from the source of heat. What we like to do sometimes is scrape any sauce that's left in the dish into a small saucepan, add the glass of white wine to it, and bring it to a boil to give some extra sauce.

Lemon Chicken Kebabs with Gremolata
Serves 4

4 boneless chicken breasts, preferably with skin on (about 6 oz each)

½ cup olive oil

Juice of 2 lemons, plus 2 teaspoons grated lemon zest

6 thick slices of lemon, cut into quarters

2 teaspoons chopped fresh oregano

2 teaspoons white wine vinegar

2 garlic cloves, crushed through a press

Salt and freshly ground black pepper to taste

4 bay leaves, torn in half

For the gremolata

2 tablespoons chopped fresh parsley

1 tablespoon grated lemon zest

2 garlic cloves, finely chopped

You will also need 4 (12-inch) wooden skewers, or use metal skewers.

Gremolata is an Italian seasoning blend — a dusting of finely chopped garlic, parsley, and lemon or orange zest that is sprinkled over cooked food just before serving. Here it adds an extra burst of flavor to lemon-marinated chunks of chicken. Serve with a nice tossed salad and buttered orzo or macaroni, sprinkled with grated cheese.

1. Begin by chopping each chicken breast into 5 chunky pieces, leaving the skin on, and place them in a bowl, along with the oil, lemon juice and zest, oregano, vinegar, garlic, and plenty of salt and pepper. Cover and leave to marinate overnight in the refrigerator for a few hours – or for as much time as you have.

2. When you are ready to cook the chicken, soak wooden skewers, if you are using them, in hot water for 30 minutes to keep them from burning. Then preheat the broiler on high at least 10 minutes ahead. Thread half a bay leaf onto the first skewer, followed by a quarter-slice of lemon, and a piece of chicken. Continue alternating the lemon and chicken until you have used 5 pieces of chicken, finishing with a lemon quarter and another half of a bay leaf at the end, and making sure you pack everything together as tightly as possible. Repeat with the remaining ingredients and skewers. Place the skewers on a broiler rack set over the broiling pan to catch the juices. Broil the kebabs 4 inches from the source of heat and, as they cook, baste them with the marinade juices (do not baste during the last 5 minutes of broiling). Cook for 10 minutes on each side, until they are dark and toasted at the edges.

3. While they're under the broiler, make the gremolata. Mix the parsley, lemon zest, and garlic together. When the skewers are done, transfer them to a serving plate and keep warm. Sprinkle the chicken with the gremolata and serve.

Triple-Mustard Deviled Chicken Thighs
Serves 4

8 chicken thighs

1 tablespoon Dijon mustard

1 tablespoon whole-grain mustard

2 tablespoons dry mustard, preferably English, mixed with 1 tablespoon hot water

2 large egg yolks

2 tablespoons heavy cream

All-purpose flour, for dusting

1 ½ cups fresh white breadcrumbs, mixed with 2 teaspoons chopped fresh mixed herbs, such as rosemary and thyme

Salt and freshly ground black pepper to taste

Peanut or other flavorless oil, for frying

A trio of piquant mustards, herbs, and a crisp breadcrumb coating fry up to the most succulent chicken thighs you've ever tasted. Great for a picnic, these are equally good hot, at room temperature, or chilled.

1. First of all, remove the skin from the chicken thighs. An incision between the skin and the thigh, using a small sharp knife, will help to pull the skin off very easily. Then, in a small bowl, mix the three mustards, egg yolks, and cream until well blended and smooth. Then place some flour on a square of waxed paper and the breadcrumb and herb mixture on another piece. Season each chicken thigh with salt and pepper and dip to coat in flour, then dip in the mustard mixture to coat it evenly, and finally, roll the pieces in the breadcrumbs and pat the coating on firmly. Place the chicken thighs on a plate. Cover and chill for 3 to 4 hours so that the mustard flavor can develop and the coating become firm.

2. Then, in a large skillet (or two smaller ones), heat about 1 inch of oil over high heat until the oil is shimmering, or to the point where a small cube of bread froths on contact. Now fry the chicken thighs on medium heat, turning them from time to time, until they're crisp and golden – 25 to 30 minutes. Drain the chicken on crumpled paper towels before serving.

Thai Coconut Chicken with Spiced Rice
Serves 4

For the chicken

1 (2.2-pound) store-bought, cooked chicken

1 teaspoon coriander seeds

½ teaspoon cumin seeds

2 cardamom pods, lightly crushed

2 tablespoons peanut or other flavorless oil

2 medium onions, finely sliced

2 garlic cloves, crushed

16 sprigs fresh cilantro

1 teaspoon ground turmeric

4 red chilies, deseeded and finely chopped

1 tablespoon finely chopped lemongrass (tender part only)

1 (14-oz) can coconut milk

2 tablespoons fresh lime juice

Salt and freshly ground black pepper to taste

For the rice

⅓ cup creamed coconut, available at Asian markets

20 sprigs fresh coriander

4 garlic cloves

2 large or 3 medium fresh green chilies

1 (1½-inch) cube fresh root ginger

1½ tablespoons peanut or other flavorless oil

3 (2-inch) pieces of cinnamon

Whether you have leftover roast chicken or pick up a rotisserie bird from the store, this is a flavor-packed recipe that's really quite special. While the ingredient list looks long, many of the ingredients in the chicken and rice are the same, and the actual cooking time is little more than half an hour.

1. To prepare the chicken, remove the skin and cut the flesh into strips about 2½ inches long. Next, the spices will need roasting, so heat one of the large skillets – without any fat in it – and, when it's really hot, add the coriander and cumin seeds and the cardamom pods. Allow the spices to roast briefly – about 45 seconds – shaking the pan from time to time, then tip them into a mortar, removing the seeds from the cardamom pods and discarding the husks, and crush the seeds all fairly finely. Now add the oil to the skillet. When it's really hot, cook the onions and garlic over medium heat for 8 to 9 minutes, until they're nicely softened. Meanwhile, strip the leaves from the cilantro stalks, reserve the whole leaves, and then chop the stalks finely.

2. For the rice, begin by dissolving the creamed coconut in 1¾ cups boiling water. Then separate the coriander leaves and stalks and finely chop the leaves to use later on. Now, place the creamed coconut mixture in a food processor with the garlic, chilies, ginger, and coriander stalks, blending until everything is finely chopped.

3. Leave this aside while you heat the oil over a gentle heat in the second skillet, then add the cinnamon pieces, cloves, peppercorns, and cashews to the skillet and sauté everything gently for about 1 minute. Next, add the onions and continue to cook over medium heat until they become softened and pale gold in color, which will take 8 to 10 minutes.

4. When the onions and garlic in the first skillet are tender, add the turmeric, chilies, crushed spices, and coriander stalks, along with the lemongrass. Stir these thoroughly together, then pour in the coconut milk and lime juice. Add some salt and pepper, then simmer everything gently for about 10 minutes, uncovered, by which time the sauce should have reduced and thickened.

5. Next, add the rice to the softened onions in the second skillet, then stir once and cook for another 2 to 3 minutes. Add the coconut liquid, give everything a stir, and

stick

6 whole cloves

15 black peppercorns

⅓ cup unsalted cashews, halved

2 medium onions, finely sliced

1½ cups basmati rice

1 cup fresh shelled peas or
thawed frozen peas

1½ teaspoons salt, or to taste

2 tablespoons fresh lime juice

You will also need two large
skillets, one with a tight-fitting lid.

cook for another 2 to 3 minutes. Now add the peas, salt, and 2 cups hot water, bring it all to a gentle simmer, then cover. Turn the heat to low and let cook very gently for 8 minutes; use a timer here, and don't lift the lid. When the rice is ready, remove the pan from the heat, take the lid off, and cover the pan with a kitchen towel for 10 minutes before serving. Finally, remove the pieces of cinnamon from the rice, sprinkle in the lime juice and the finely chopped coriander leaves, then fluff the rice gently with a fork.

6. Meanwhile, add the chicken to the thickened coconut sauce and simmer gently for 10 minutes or so to heat it through completely. Serve the chicken on a bed of rice, garnished with the reserved whole cilantro leaves.

Curried Chicken Salad with Almonds, Raisins, and Apricots
Serves 6

⅓ cup whole blanched almonds

1 (2.2-pound) store-bought, cooked chicken or 3 cups (about 1 pound) leftover chicken meat

⅓ cup mayonnaise

¼ cup plain lowfat yogurt

1 tablespoon mango chutney with any bits of mango finely chopped

½ tablespoon Madras-style curry powder

⅓ cup raisins

⅓ cup dried apricots, quartered

3 scallions, white and green parts

Salt and freshly ground black pepper to taste

6 cups baby greens or mesclun

1 tablespoon fresh cilantro leaves, to garnish

This is unbelievably easy if you buy ready-cooked chicken. It's also a great way of using up leftover chicken and is perfect for serving as part of a buffet.

1. Preheat the oven to 350°F. Spread the almonds out on a baking sheet and toast in the oven for 8 minutes, using a timer. Let them cool for a couple of minutes, then roughly chop them.

2. Now, if using a whole chicken, strip all the meat from it, discarding the skin and bones. Cut the chicken into bite-sized pieces and place them in a mixing bowl. Then, in a small bowl, mix the mayonnaise and yogurt with mango chutney and curry, then pour this dressing over the chicken. Next, add the raisins, apricots, about two-thirds of the almonds and about three-quarters of the scallions. Mix everything together thoroughly, taste and season with salt and freshly ground black pepper, then cover and chill until needed.

3. When you are ready to serve, place the salad leaves in the base of a serving dish and spoon the chicken over the top, heaping it up to give it some height. Then scatter the remaining almonds and scallions and the cilantro leaves over the top.

Roast Chicken with Grape Stuffing and Gravy
Serves 4

For the stuffing

7 tablespoons butter

1 medium onion, finely chopped

2 ½ cups fresh breadcrumbs

1 cup seedless grapes, halved

4 garlic cloves, crushed through a press

1 tablespoon chopped fresh parsley

2 teaspoons chopped fresh tarragon

Salt and freshly ground black pepper to taste

For the chicken

1 (4-pound) chicken

Salt and freshly ground black pepper to taste

4 tablespoons butter, at room temperature

For the gravy

1 ½ tablespoons all-purpose flour

1 ¼ cups dry white wine

1 ¼ cups chicken stock, such as Chicken Giblet Stock (see page 127)

Salt and freshly ground black pepper to taste

This is good for a family Sunday lunch in summer with fresh, shelled, broad green beans and buttered new potatoes.

1. First, preheat the oven 375°F. Meanwhile, make the stuffing. Melt 1 tablespoon of the butter in a small saucepan and cook the onion for about 5 minutes or until softened, then add the remaining 6 tablespoons of butter and allow it to melt. Now transfer the onion and the buttery juices to a bowl, add the breadcrumbs, then stir in the grapes, garlic, parsley, and tarragon. Taste and season with salt and pepper.

2. Next, loosen the breast skin of the chicken a little to make a pocket for the stuffing. Place the stuffing in the pocket but don't overfill – if you do, the skin will burst when cooking. Secure the skin flap underneath with a small skewer. Season the chicken all over with lots of salt and pepper, then rub it all over with the butter, and cover the breast with buttered aluminum foil.

3. Place the chicken on a rack in a roasting pan and cook for approximately 1 hour, 20 minutes, basting the meat with the buttery juices every 20 minutes or so. Remove the foil about 30 minutes before the end of the cooking time to brown the breast. To test if the chicken is cooked, pierce the thickest part of the thigh with a thin skewer: if cooked, the juices will run golden and clear. Drain the chicken thoroughly and keep warm while you make the gravy.

4. Carefully tilt the roasting pan and pour off some of the excess fat – you need to leave about 1 to 1 ½ tablespoons of fat behind. Then put the pan over direct low heat turned fairly low when the juices begin to sizzle, and blend in the flour. Keep stirring and allow the flour to brown before gradually adding the wine and the stock to make a thin gravy. Taste and season with salt and pepper. Carve the chicken and serve, passing the gravy separately.

Baked Chicken with Garlic and Parmesan Cheese
Serves 4

1 (3½-pound) chicken, cut into 8 pieces, or 4 leg quarters

4 large garlic cloves

Sea salt, as needed

2 large eggs

Freshly ground black pepper to taste

4 tablespoons butter

4 tablespoons olive oil

1¼ cups fresh breadcrumbs

⅓ cup (1½ oz) freshly grated Parmesan cheese

3 tablespoons finely chopped fresh parsley

You will also need a roasting pan large enough to hold the chicken in one layer.

While included in the summer section, because it's so good as picnic fare, this succulent, Italian-inspired chicken is really an evergreen recipe, perfect any time of year. Marinated, coated, and baked until golden brown, it's one dish the whole family will love.

1. First of all, arrange the chicken pieces in a shallow dish in a single layer to marinate. Then place the garlic cloves in a mortar with 1¼ teaspoons salt and crush the garlic to a purée. Now add this to the eggs in a bowl, season with some pepper, and whisk well with a fork before pouring it over the chicken. Cover the dish with plastic wrap and refrigerate for a minimum of 4 hours, turning the chicken over halfway through.

2. Preheat the oven to 350°F. Place the roasting pan containing the butter and oil into the oven to melt the butter and heat the fats as well. Meanwhile, combine the breadcrumbs with the Parmesan, parsley, and a little salt and pepper together on a plate. Spread out some paper towels. Remove the chicken from the refrigerator, take one piece at a time and carefully sit it in the crumb mixture, patting and coating it all over with crumbs (trying not to disturb the egg and garlic already clinging to it).

3. Next, remove the pan with the hot fat in it from the oven and add the chicken pieces. Baste well and bake on a high oven rack for 20 minutes. Then turn the chicken pieces over and give them another 20 minutes. Finally, pouring off the excess fat from the pan and give them another 5 minutes. Drain them on more paper towels, leave to cool. When cooled, wrap the pieces individually in aluminum foil for transportation.

Tandoori-Style Chicken Kebabs with Cilantro Chutney
Serves 4

For the marinade

1 teaspoon cumin seeds

1 ½ teaspoons coriander seeds

12 cardamom pods

4 teaspoons each turmeric and grated fresh ginger

3 garlic cloves, crushed

½ teaspoon sea salt

4 boneless chicken breasts, preferably with skin on (about 6 oz each)

1 tablespoon peanut or other flavorless oil

1 ¼ cups plain lowfat yogurt

For the fresh cilantro chutney

1 ½ cup packed cilantro leaves

2 tablespoons fresh lime juice

1 fresh green chili, halved and deseeded

1 garlic clove

½ teaspoon sugar

For the kebabs

4 fresh bay leaves, cut in half

½ large red onion, halved and separated into 8 pieces

8 fresh green chilies, halved and deseeded

Salt and freshly ground black pepper to taste

Olive oil, for sprinkling

Lime quarters, for serving

You will also need 4 (12-inch) wooden or metal skewers

Yogurt as a marinade does wonders for chicken, making it deliciously tender. This is great barbecue food – the charcoal really does add an extra dimension – but these kebabs can also be grilled very successfully. Serve with raw red onion and tomato salad.

1. For the marinade, dry-roast the cumin and coriander seeds and the cardamom pods in a small pan over medium heat for about 1 minute, or until the seeds begin to jump. When they have cooled, remove the seeds from the cardamom pods and, using a pestle and mortar, crush them with the cumin and coriander seeds. Next, add the turmeric, ginger, garlic, and salt and mix everything well.

2. Now cut each chicken breast into 5 pieces, place them in a bowl, and toss first in oil, then in the spice mixture, mixing everything around so it gets an even coating. Next, add all but 1 tablespoon of the yogurt (reserve this for the chutney). Give everything a good stir and press the chicken pieces down into the marinade. Cover with plastic wrap pressed onto the surface, and refrigerate for a few hours or overnight.

3. To make the chutney, simply purée everything, including the reserved 1 tablespoon yogurt, together in a blender, then pour into a bowl and set aside for 2 to 3 hours to allow the flavors to develop.

4. When you are almost ready to cook the kebabs, if you're using wooden skewers, soak them in hot water for 30 minutes (to prevent them from burning). Light the barbecue or preheat the broiler to its highest setting for 10 minutes. Thread half a bay leaf on to a skewer, then a piece of chicken, a piece of onion, and half a chili. Carry on alternating the chicken, onion, and chili until you have used up 5 pieces of chicken per kebab, and finish with half a bay leaf. Make sure you pack everything as tightly as possible, then season, lay the kebabs on a rack, and sprinkle with a little olive oil. Line the broiler pan with foil, place the rack on top, and arrange the kebabs on the rack. Broil the kebabs for 10 minutes on each side, about 4 inches away from the source of the heat, or simply grill over a barbecue. To serve, slip the chicken off the skewers, using a fork to ease the pieces off (and a cloth to protect your hand), and serve, garnished with lime quarters, and the chutney passed separately.

Chicken Sauté with Shallots, Sherry Vinegar, and Tarragon
Serves 4

2 tablespoons olive oil

1 (3½-pound) chicken, cut into 8 pieces, or 4 chicken breasts with skin and bone

Salt and freshly ground black pepper to taste

12 shallots, peeled

4 garlic cloves, peeled

2 tablespoons fresh tarragon leaves, plus 8 small sprigs of fresh tarragon, to garnish

⅔ cup sherry vinegar

1¾ cups medium-dry Amontillado sherry

1½ tablespoons crème fraîche

You will also need a large, roomy skillet, 9 inches in diameter.

This is an adaptation of a classic French dish called *poulet au vinaigre*. It's very simple to make: the sautéed chicken is flavored with tarragon and simmered uncovered in a mixture of medium-dry sherry and sherry vinegar along with lightly browned whole shallots and cloves of garlic until the liquid cooks down to glossy, concentrated sauce. Serve with parslied potatoes and a simple vegetable.

1. First of all, heat the oil in the skillet and season the chicken with salt and pepper. Then, when the oil begins to shimmer, fry the chicken in two batches to brown well: remove the first batch to a plate while you tackle the second. Each piece needs to be a lovely golden brown color. When the second batch is ready, remove it to the plate to join the rest. Then add the shallots to the pan, brown these a little, and finally, add the garlic cloves to color slightly.

2. Now turn the heat down, return the chicken to the pan, scatter the tarragon leaves all over, then pour in the vinegar and sherry. Let it all simmer for a bit, then turn the heat to very low, so that the whole thing barely bubbles, for 45 minutes. Halfway through, turn the chicken pieces over to allow the other sides to sit in the sauce. When they're cooked through, remove them to a warm serving dish, right side up, along with the shallots and garlic.

3. The sauce will by now have reduced and concentrated, so all you do is whisk the crème fraîche into it, taste it, and season as required, then pour the sauce all over the chicken and scatter with the sprigs of tarragon.

Roast Chicken with Lemon Sauce
Serves 4

For the sauce

1 ¼ cups chicken stock, such as Chicken Giblet Stock (see page 127)

1 tablespoon all-purpose flour

Grated zest of ½ lemon

1 tablespoon fresh lemon juice

⅔ cup crème fraîche

For the chicken

1 (4-pound) chicken

6 tablespoons softened butter

Salt, as needed

Freshly ground black pepper to taste

1 lemon, plus 1 tablespoons fresh lemon juice

1 teaspoon chopped fresh tarragon

You will also need a heavy 9- x 13-inch flameproof roasting pan.

How surprising that a simple lemon can make what is already an impeccably fine, comforting dish, even better. Since the entire fruit, peel, and all goes inside the chicken, look for organic lemons. Otherwise, be sure to scrub the fruit well with soap and water before using.

1. First of all, reduce the stock down to ⅔ cup to give a concentrated flavor. This should be done in a wide saucepan, without a lid, boiling vigorously.

2. Preheat the oven to 400°F. Next, prepare the chicken for roasting by mixing the butter with ¼ teaspoon of salt, some freshly ground pepper, and the lemon juice. Add the tarragon, then spread this mixture evenly all over the chicken. Now cut the lemon into quarters and place these inside the chicken. Next, place the chicken in a roasting pan and cover the breast with buttered foil. Roast for 1¼-1½ hours, basting the chicken quite often with the buttery juices. Remove the foil from the breast during the last half hour.

3. When the chicken is ready (the juices in the thigh should run clear when pierced with a skewer), transfer the chicken to a warm plate and cover with aluminum foil. While the chicken is "relaxing" you can make the sauce. Tilt the roasting pan and remove most of the fat, which you will see separates quite clearly from the juices – you need to leave behind about 2 tablespoons.

4. Now place the roasting pan over fairly low heat, and when the juices begin to sizzle, blend in the flour and stir vigorously until you have a smooth paste and then gradually add the reduced stock, lemon zest and juice. Bring to the boil, stirring all the time, simmer for 2 to 3 minutes. Then add the crème fraîche and season to taste with salt and pepper. Carve the chicken and serve with the sauce poured over.

Autumn

Baked Chicken Legs Glazed with Maple Barbeque Sauce
Serves 4

1 tablespoon olive oil

1 tablespoon fresh lemon juice

4 chicken thighs and 4 drumsticks, or 1 (3½-pound) chicken, cut into 8 pieces

1 medium onion, finely chopped

Salt and freshly ground black pepper to taste

For the sauce

⅓ cup hearty red wine

¼ cup Japanese soy sauce

2 tablespoons red wine vinegar

2 tablespoons pure maple syrup

1½ tablespoons tomato paste

1½ teaspoons ground ginger

1½ teaspoons dry mustard

2 garlic cloves, crushed

1½ teaspoons hot red pepper sauce

To finish

¼ cup hearty red wine

A few sprigs of watercress, for garnish

You will also need a 9- x 13-inch, flameproof roasting pan.

Although the chicken takes about 50 minutes to cook, there is actually very little work involved here. Baking the chicken first until it is almost cooked through ensures the sauce will not burn.

1. First, mix the olive oil with the lemon juice. Place the chicken in the roasting pan with the chopped onion tucked among them. Season with a little salt and freshly ground black pepper. Brush the chicken pieces with the oil and lemon juice.

2. When you're ready to cook the chicken, preheat the oven to 400°F. Place the pan on a high rack of the oven and let it cook for 25 minutes exactly.

3. Meanwhile, whisk all of the sauce ingredients in a bowl. Then, when the 25 minutes are up, remove the chicken from the oven, pour off any surplus fat from the corner of the pan, and pour the sauce all over, giving everything a good coating. Now back it goes into the oven for about another 25 minutes (you will need to baste it twice during this time), until the chicken shows no sign of pink when pierced at the bone. After that, remove the roasting pan from the oven and place it over medium heat.

4. Then pour in the final ¼ cup red wine, stir it into the sauce, let it just bubble for about 1 minute. Serve the chicken with the sauce spooned over. Garnish with a few sprigs of watercress.

Puff Pastry Chicken Pies
Serves 4

For the filling

1 pound boneless and skinless chicken thighs

2 tablespoons butter

1 small onion, finely chopped

4 bacon slices, cut into ¼-inch wide strips

3 tablespoons all-purpose flour

1¼ cups chicken broth

6 cremini mushrooms, finely sliced

Salt and freshly ground black pepper to taste

¼ cup heavy cream or crème fraîche

1½ tablespoons finely chopped fresh parsley

For the pastry

1 17.3-oz box of frozen puff pastry, thawed

2 large egg yolks, beaten

You will also need a lightly buttered rimmed baking sheet, and a ruler.

Convenient, ready-made sheets of puff pastry, sold in the frozen-food section of supermarkets, make decorative savory pastries like this one easy to make. They are elegant enough to serve at a supper party and need only a good salad or simple green vegetable as accompaniment.

1. First of all, you need to trim the chicken into even-sized pieces – roughly ½-inch cubes. Then melt the butter in a medium, deep-sided skillet and cook the chopped onion over medium heat until it has turned pale gold – about 4 minutes. Then, using a slotted spoon, transfer it to a plate. Now turn the heat to high and add the bacon strips and cook these, tossing them around a few times, for about 4 minutes, until they are really crisp. After that, transfer the bacon to the onion and start to cook the chicken in the bacon fat. You'll need to do this in three batches, and each batch should take about 3-4 minutes to turn golden on all sides. Now return the onion and bacon and all the chicken to the skillet. Then, using a wooden spoon, and reducing the heat to medium, sprinkle in the flour and stir it in to soak up all the juices.

2. After that, add the chicken broth a little at a time, stirring as you add until all the broth has been incorporated. Then, as it comes to simmer, it will have thickened to a creamy sauce. At this stage, add the mushrooms, season well, and then let it simmer at the lowest possible heat, uncovered, for 30 minutes, giving it a stir from time to time. Finally, stir in the cream and the parsley, taste to check the seasoning. Set aside until it is completely cooled, then cover and refrigerate. All this can be done well ahead of time.

3. When you want to bake the pies, preheat the oven to 400°F. Roll out 1 pastry sheet until it measures 14- x 9½-inches. Trim 2½ inches off the long side, then cut into two 7- x 7-inch squares. Repeat with the remaining pastry sheet. Gather up the trimmings and refrigerate until later. Roll out each pastry until it is about 8 inches square. Now divide the cold filling among the 4 pieces of pastry, placing it in the center. Next, brush the edges with the beaten egg yolk, pull up the 4 opposite corners to

meet in the center so what you have resembles 4 envelopes. Then pinch the seams together carefully, as you don't want them to burst open. Now make a small hole in the center of each one to allow the steam to escape during baking. Re-roll the pastry trimmings quite thinly and cut them into leaf shapes, making veins in the leaves with the back of a knife. Then arrange the leaves to decorate the parcels. Place the pies on a greased baking sheet. You can make the pies up to this stage a few hours in advance and chill them.

4. Brush the pies thickly with beaten egg yolk. Bake on a high rack in the oven for 20 to 25 minutes, or until they are a rich golden brown.

Chicken with Roasted Lemon, Red Onion, Garlic, and Thyme
Serves 4

1 (3½-pound) chicken

2 tablespoons olive oil

1 large red onion, peeled and cut into 6 wedges through the root

1 large lemon, quartered, plus a squeeze of lemon juice for the sauce

6 garlic cloves (no need to peel them)

Salt and freshly ground black pepper to taste

1 tablespoon fresh thyme leaves and a few small sprigs

1¼ cups dry white wine

2 tablespoons crème fraîche or heavy cream

You will also need a flameproof roasting pan, about 9- x 13-inches.

Something lovely happens to lemons when they're roasted – they lose some of their sharp edge and taste more mellow. Here they're served, along with the mellow roasted garlic cloves, as an edible garnish. Serve with mashed potatoes and parsnips and steamed broccoli.

1. Begin by taking the chicken from the refrigerator about an hour before you intend to cook it (if it's a hot day, give it about 30 minutes only). This will take the chill off the bird and help it to cook in the shorter time. Preheat the oven to 400°F.

2. Now put 1 tablespoon of the olive oil in the roasting pan and toss the onion, lemon, and garlic in it. Then push everything to the sides of the pan and place the chicken in the middle. Rub remaining 1 tablespoon of the olive oil all over the skin. Then arrange the onion wedges, lemon, and garlic cloves around the chicken.

3. Season well with salt and black pepper and then scatter the thyme leaves and the small sprigs of thyme over everything in the pan. Now roast the chicken for about 1¼ hours, basting it once or twice, until the juices run clear when pierced with a skewer near the thigh. Then transfer it to a carving board, along with the red onions, lemon, and garlic. Cover it with aluminum foil and let it rest for 20 minutes.

4. Meanwhile, using a tablespoon, skim off the excess fat from the juices in the roasting pan, then place the pan over high heat. Add the wine and let the it boil and reduce to about half its original volume. Stir the crème fraîche in next, adding a small squeeze of lemon juice, bring it back to the simmer, and taste and check the seasoning. Then carve the chicken and place it on warm plates, making sure everyone has a piece of onion and lemon and some garlic. Add any carving juices to the sauce, spoon some sauce over the chicken, and serve the leftover sauce in a sauceboat. You can squeeze the garlic pulp out of the cloves as you eat it, and scrape off the lemony flesh from the skins.

Chicken Breasts in Zesty Tomato Sauce with Olives, Capers, and Fresh Basil
Serves 4

2 tablespoons extra virgin olive oil

4 chicken breasts with skin and bone (7 to 8 oz each)

Salt and freshly ground black pepper to taste

2 garlic cloves, crushed

1 fresh red chili, deseeded and finely chopped

1 (14-oz) can chopped tomatoes, preferably Italian

1 ½ tablespoons tomato paste

1 cup pitted black olives, roughly chopped

1 ½ tablespoons capers, rinsed and drained

1 tablespoon chopped fresh basil, plus a few extra sprigs as garnish

12 ounces dried spinach fettuccine, for serving

You will need a very large skillet.

This is a take-off on a quick pasta sauce, called *puttanesca*. It's a lovely, gutsy sauce that is also extremely good with chicken that's been sautéed first, then gently simmered in the sauce to absorb all the flavors. No need to miss out on the pasta either, as green tagliatelle is the perfect accompaniment.

1. Begin by heating the oil in the skillet. Wipe the chicken breasts with paper towels, season them with salt and pepper. Add them to the hot oil and cook over medium heat until they are a rich golden color on both sides. This will take about 5 or 6 minutes. Then transfer the chicken to a plate and add the garlic and chili to the pan and cook briefly for about 30 seconds.

2. After that, add the tomatoes, tomato paste, olives, capers, chopped basil, and some seasoning. Stir everything well, bring to a gentle simmer, then return the chicken breasts to the pan, skin side up, pushing them well down into the sauce and basting a little over the top. Now simmer for 40 to 45 minutes, uncovered, until the chicken has cooked through and the sauce has reduced and thickened.

3. Meanwhile, bring a large pot of salted water to a boil over high heat. Just before the chicken is done, add the fettuccine and cook until al dente (barely tender). Quickly drain the pasta. Serve the chicken with the sauce spooned over, the tagliatelle on the side, and garnish with the fresh sprigs of basil.

Chicken Sauté with Melting Onions, Fresh Tomatoes, and Rosemary
Serves 4

1 tablespoon olive oil

1 (3½-pound) chicken, cut into 8 pieces

Salt and freshly ground black pepper to taste

2 large onions, thickly sliced

1½ pounds ripe tomatoes

2 large garlic cloves, crushed through a press

1¼ cups dry white wine

1 tablespoon white wine vinegar

1 tablespoon tomato paste

1 tablespoon fresh rosemary leaves, bruised and finely chopped, plus a few small sprigs

1 bay leaf

You will also need a medium flameproof casserole with a lid.

Perfect for early autumn, when your garden — or local farmer's market — is laden with juicy red, ripe tomatoes, bursting with flavor. Serve with rice or noodles and a simple green vegetable.

1. First of all, heat the oil in the casserole over high heat and season the chicken with salt and pepper. Then, when the oil gets really hot and begins to shimmer, fry the chicken – in two batches – to brown it well on all sides: remove the first batch to a plate while you tackle the second; each piece needs to be a lovely golden brown color all over. When the second batch is ready, remove it to join the rest. Now add the onions to the casserole, turn the heat down to medium, and cook for 8 to 10 minutes, or until they are softened and nicely browned at the edges.

2. Meanwhile, skin the tomatoes. To do this, pour boiling water over them and leave them for exactly 1 minute before draining and slipping off their skins (protect your hands with a cloth if they are too hot), then chop them quite small.

3. When the onions are browned, add the garlic to the casserole, let this cook for about 1 minute. Then add the tomatoes, wine, vinegar, tomato paste, rosemary, and bay leaf. Now add some seasoning and bring it to a boil. Let cook a steady simmer (without covering) and reduce to about half its original volume, which will take about 20 minutes. Now add the chicken, stir them around a bit, then put the lid on and simmer gently for 40 minutes, until the chicken is cooked through.

Chicken Medallions Stuffed with Wild Mushrooms in Marsala Sauce
Serves 4

½ ounce dried porcini mushrooms

2 tablespoons butter, plus extra for the foil

3 ounces sliced bacon or pancetta

1 medium onion, finely chopped

6 ounces shiitake mushrooms, stemmed and finely chopped

1 plump garlic clove, crushed

1½ teaspoons chopped fresh sage leaves

A grating of fresh nutmeg

Salt and freshly ground black pepper to taste

4 boneless and skinless chicken breasts (about 5 oz each)

For the sauce

1 teaspoon peanut or other flavorless oil

Reserved chopped bacon

1 shallot, chopped

3 small button mushrooms, finely sliced

1 teaspoon chopped fresh sage leaves

1 tablespoon all-purpose flour

Soaking liquid from porcini

⅔ cup dry Marsala, plus more as needed

Salt and freshly ground black pepper to taste

You will also need 4 (10-inch) aluminum foil squares.

Because these delectable stuffed chicken breasts are fully formed and then chilled thoroughly before being cooked, they are extremely adaptable for entertaining: no last-minute fuss.

1. First, soak the porcini mushrooms, so place them a small bowl, pour ⅔ cup boiling water over them, and soak for 20 minutes. After that, strain them in a sieve placed over a bowl and squeeze every last bit of liquid out of them into a bowl because you are going to need it for the sauce. Now melt the butter in a skillet. Finely chop the bacon or pancetta and cook half of it in the hot butter until golden and crisp, and transfer it to a plate. Then add the onion to the pan and cook gently for about 5 minutes to soften.

2. While that is happening, rinse and finely chop the porcini. Add them to the skillet, along with the shiitakes, reserved bacon, garlic, and sage, and a little nutmeg. Stir well to get everything coated with the butter, then, as soon as the juices start to run out of the mushrooms, reduce the heat to very low and cook gently, without covering, until all the juices have evaporated and you have a thick mushroom paste, about 30 minutes in all. After that, remove it from the heat, taste, and season well with salt and freshly ground black pepper, then allow it to cool completely.

3. Now take each of the chicken breasts and cut out the silvery tendon from the underside. Make a deep cut in the thickest part of the breast and fold it back so it opens out, almost like a book, and season the chicken. Next, spread a quarter of the mushroom mixture over one of the breasts, and roll it up lengthways. When they are all filled, lay each chicken breast on a lightly buttered piece of foil. Wrap each in its foil, folding over the ends to seal. At this stage the parcels should be chilled for at least an hour to firm up.

4. When you're ready to cook them, preheat the oven to 450°F. Place the parcels on a baking sheet and cook for 20 minutes. Then remove them from the oven and allow them to rest in the foil for 10 minutes before serving.

5. While the chicken is cooking, make the sauce. First heat the oil in the skillet. Add the reserved bacon to the skillet with the shallot, and cook for about

5 minutes. Add the mushrooms and sage, stir, and continue to cook for about 1 minute, by which time the juices of the mushrooms will begin to run.

6. Next, stir in the flour to soak up the juices, then gradually add the porcini-soaking liquid, followed by the Marsala, and give a good seasoning of salt and pepper. Keep stirring until the sauce comes to a boil and thickens. Turn the heat down and, if you think the sauce is too thick, add a spoonful more of Marsala. Now let the sauce cook very gently for about 20 minutes. To serve, unwrap each parcel on to a plate and cut each into 4 pieces at an angle to show the stuffing. Then pour the sauce over or around each one and serve immediately.

Cider-Braised Chicken with Mushrooms and Bacon
Serves 4

2 tablespoons peanut or other flavorless oil

1 (3½-pound) chicken, cut into 8 pieces

Salt and freshly ground black pepper to taste

2 medium onions, chopped

1 garlic clove, chopped

6 slices bacon

1 sprig of fresh thyme

1 bay leaf

2 cups hard cider or 1 cup each apple juice and dry white wine

8 ounces cremini mushrooms, sliced

3 tablespoons all-purpose flour mashed with 2 tablespoons softened butter to make a paste

You will also need a 4 quart flameproof casserole with a lid.

The natural sweetness of apple cider provides the perfect balance to salty bacon and earthy mushrooms in this easy stew. It is particularly good served with buttered new potatoes and braised red cabbage.

1. First of all, heat the oil in the casserole over high heat and season the chicken with salt and pepper. Then, when the oil gets really hot and begins to shimmer, add the chicken in two batches to brown it well on all sides. Transfer the first batch to a plate while you tackle the second; each piece needs to be a lovely golden brown color all over. When the second batch is ready, transfer it to join the rest.

2. Now cook the onions and garlic for 5 minutes or so. Next, add the bacon, which should be cooked to melt the fat a little. Then return everything to the casserole. Throw in the thyme and bay leaf, and pour in the cider. Bring it all to a simmer, then cover with the lid. Simmer gently for 1 hour. At the end of that time add the mushrooms and simmer for a further 5-7 minutes or until the mushrooms are cooked and the chicken is cooked through.

3. Have ready the flour-butter paste. When the chicken is cooked, using a slotted spoon, transfer the chicken to a warm serving dish. Next, whisk the paste into the liquid and bring back to simmering point, whisking all the time. Pour the thickened sauce over the chicken and serve immediately.

Thai Green Curry Chicken
Serves 4-6

For the green curry paste

6 to 8 whole green bird's-eye or serrano chiles

1 lemongrass stalk, tender part thinly sliced and soaked for 30 minutes in 2 tablespoons lime juice

5 shallots, preferably Thai, peeled

1½ teaspoons chopped fresh cilantro stalks

1½ teaspoons thinly shredded lime zest, preferably kaffir lime

1 (1-inch) piece peeled fresh galangal or ginger

½ teaspoon each ground cumin and coriander seeds, pan-toasted and ground

3 garlic cloves

1 teaspoon shrimp paste

For the chicken curry

2 (14-oz) cans coconut milk (you will only need 1½ tins for the recipe; you can freeze the leftover amount for use later on)

3 tablespoons Thai fish sauce

1 teaspoon light brown or palm sugar

3 cups (1 pound) cooked and thinly shredded chicken

2 tablespoons green peppercorns in brine, drained

7 kaffir lime leaves, optional

½ moderately hot red chile, such as jalapeño, deseeded and thinly shredded

20 fresh basil leaves, preferably Thai, torn

What better use of leftover cooked chicken than in this savory dish? The unique flavors of Thai cooking are so simple – and you can also use a good-quality cooked chicken from the supermarket. Serve over steamed jasmine rice.

1. The curry paste can be made well ahead of time and there's almost no work involved if you have a food processor or a blender because all you do is simply add all of the ingredients into the container and process them into a paste (stopping once or twice to push the mixture back down from the sides on to the blades). In Thailand, of course, all these would be pounded by hand with a pestle and mortar, but food processors do cut out all the hard work. What you need to end up with is a coarse paste, but don't worry if it doesn't look very green – that's because I have cut the chili content; in Thailand they use about 35! If you want yours to be green, then this is the answer. Your next task is to prepare all the rest of the ingredients.

2. To make the curry, first place the cans of coconut milk upside down on a work surface. Open them and inside you will see the whole thing has separated into thick cream and thin watery milk. Divide these by pouring the milk into one bowl and the cream into another. Place a large flameproof casserole or a wok, without any oil in it, over a very high heat and then as soon as it becomes hot, add three-quarters of the thick coconut cream. What you do now is literally fry it, stirring all the time so it doesn't stick. What will happen is it will start to separate, the oil will begin to seep out and it will reduce. Ignore the curdled look – this is normal. You may also like to note that when the cream begins to separate you can actually hear it give off a crackling noise.

3. Next, add the curry paste and three-quarters of the coconut milk, which should be added a little at a time, keeping the heat high and letting it reduce slightly. Stay with it and keep stirring to prevent it sticking. Then stir in the fish sauce and sugar, and then add the chicken and peppercorns. Stir again and simmer everything for 4 or 5 minutes until the chicken is heated through. Then just before serving, place the lime leaves, if using, one on top of the other, roll them up tightly and slice them into very fine shreds. Add them, along with the red chili and torn basil leaves.

Crunchy Pistachio-Crusted Drumsticks
Serves 4

8 chicken drumsticks, skin removed

3 tablespoons peanut or other flavorless oil

1½ tablespoons fresh lemon juice

¾ cup all-purpose flour

1½ tablespoons Madras-style curry powder

¼ teaspoon salt

Freshly ground black pepper to taste

1 cup (4 oz) shelled pistachio nuts

1 tablespoon fresh cilantro leaves

Pinch of cayenne pepper

1 large egg, beaten

3 tablespoons milk

You will also need a rimmed baking sheet.

This recipe also works very well using salted peanuts instead of the pistachios. The chicken has a crunchy coating with a slightly oriental flavor and is popular with both children and adults. This recipe is best started the day before you want to eat the chicken, so it has time to marinate.

1. First of all, marinate the chicken. Place the drumsticks in a dish. Mix 1½ tablespoons of the oil and the lemon juice together and pour this over the chicken. Then refrigerate and marinate the drumsticks for at least one hour or overnight, if you have the time, turning them over once or twice during this period.

2. To make the coating, mix the flour, curry powder, salt and pepper together in a shallow dish. When you are ready to cook, a few at a time, toss the drumsticks in the flour mixture until well coated on all sides. Tap off the surplus flour, then place them on a plate, reserving the unused flour for later.

3. Now preheat the oven to 350°F. Place the pistachios, cilantro, 1½ tablespoons of the reserved flour, and the cayenne in a food processor and blend until you have a mixture chopped minutely small, then transfer this to a plate.

4. After that, beat the egg and milk together in a bowl. Then take each drumstick and dip it once more in the remaining seasoned flour, then into the egg mixture, and finally, into the pistachio mixture. Return the coated drumsticks to their plate and keep cool until needed.

5. To cook, place the baking sheet containing the remaining 1½ tablespoons of oil in the oven to heat until hot. Add the drumsticks to the hot oil (making sure they don't touch each other), baste well, and bake on a high oven rack for 35 minutes. Then pour off the oil, turn the oven up to 425°F, and bake them 5 more minutes to get really crisp. Drain on paper towels and serve.

Chicken Saltimbocca
Serves 4

2 boneless and skinless chicken breasts (about 6 oz each)

Salt and freshly ground black pepper to taste

2 slices prosciutto (not too thinly sliced)

4 large fresh sage leaves

1 cup dry Marsala

2 teaspoons olive oil

You will also need 4 wooden toothpicks.

Saltimbocca is a classic Italian dish, which is usually made with thin veal but it also works beautifully with chicken. The chicken is quickly sautéed and then the whole thing is finished with a rich, dark Marsala wine sauce.

1. First of all, prepare the chicken breasts, which need to be flattened out. So, place one of them between 2 large pieces of plastic wrap and gently pound it, using a rolling pin, being careful not to break the meat. It needs to be flattened out until it is about 6 x 7 inches, and roughly $\frac{1}{8}$ inch thick. Repeat this with the remaining chicken breast, using fresh plastic wrap as needed. Now cut each flattened chicken breast into 2 pieces about 3- x 3½-inches each for 4 pieces total. Season the chicken with salt and pepper.

2. Next, you need to cut the prosciutto into 4 pieces. Don't worry if some of the pieces fall apart, as they can be patched together during the next step. Now place a piece of prosciutto on top of each piece of chicken, folding and creasing the prosciutto to fit the chicken as needed. Finally, top each one with a sage leaf and secure the whole thing together with a toothpick.

3. Next, measure the Marsala into a small saucepan and heat it gently until it begins to simmer. While that's happening, cook the chicken. Heat the oil in a large skillet over fairly high heat and when it's really hot, put in the pieces of chicken, sage side down. Reduce the heat to medium and cook for 2 to 3 minutes, until crisp and golden. Then turn them over and give the other side a minute or so (until the chicken feels firm when pressed in the center) before transferring to a warm serving dish.

4. Now pour the warmed Marsala into the skillet, turn the heat to high, and let it boil and reduce to a syrupy sauce, which should take about 5 minutes. Return the chicken pieces to the pan and turn in the sauce. Serve on warmed plates (not forgetting to remove the toothpicks!) with the sauce poured over.

Chicken Waldorf Salad
Serves 4

1 pound cooked chicken, torn into longish shreds about 1 inch thick (about 1 pound)

2 celery ribs, chopped

1 Granny Smith green apple, peeled, cored, and sliced

4 scallions, white and green parts, chopped

½ cup (2 oz) walnuts, coarsely chopped

1 head green leaf lettuce, separated into leaves

½ cup seedless red grapes, halved, for garnish

Watercress, for garnish (optional)

For the dressing

1 teaspoon sea salt

2 garlic cloves

3 tablespooons mayonnaise

3 tablespoons plain lowfat yogurt

2 teaspoons chopped fresh tarragon

Freshly ground black pepper to taste

An American classic is updated here with grapes in addition to the apple and lightened with yogurt in addition to the mayonnaise. Serve on a bed of crisp lettuce with plenty of crusty peasant bread as a lovely main-course salad.

1. Place the chicken in a large bowl. Next, add the celery and apple, along with the scallions and chopped walnuts.

2. Now for the dressing. Place the salt in a mortar and crush it quite coarsely, then add the garlic and, as you begin to crush it and it comes into contact with the salt, it will quickly break down to a purée. Next add the mayonnaise, yogurt, and tarragon, with a few twists of freshly ground pepper and blend everything together thoroughly.

3. Pour the dressing over the chicken mixture and toss everything together well to get a good coating of the dressing. Arrange some lettuce leaves in a large, shallow serving dish, pile the chicken salad on top, sprinkle the grapes all over, and, if you like, garnish with sprigs of watercress.

Double-Ginger Baked Chicken Breasts
Serves 4

2 tablespoons peanut or other flavorless oil

1 large onion, finely chopped

2 garlic cloves, crushed

4 chicken breasts with skin and bone (about 7 oz each)

¼ cup preserved stem ginger syrup (drained from jar of preserved ginger)

2 teaspoons grated fresh ginger

Salt and freshly ground black pepper to taste

2 tablespoons butter, cut into 4 slices

½ cup dry white wine or hard cider

4 pieces of preserved stem ginger in syrup (available at specialty grocers and Asian markets), removed from its syrup and finely chopped

2 tablespoons plain lowfat yogurt

4 scallions, white and green parts, finely sliced on the diagonal, for garnish

Preserved stem ginger along with grated fresh ginger packs a wallop that will delight ginger lovers. It's an easy oven dish that's good with a pungent salad of watercress, arugula, and baby spinach. A mix of white and wild rice would also not be amiss.

1. Start off by preheating the oven to 375°F. Heat the oil in a medium saucepan and soften the onion and garlic in it for about 5 minutes. Meanwhile, place the chicken breasts in a roasting pan just large enough to hold them comfortably. Then pierce the chicken with a skewer or small sharp knife in several places to allow the syrup to seep down inside.

2. Now spoon the ginger syrup over the chicken, rubbing it in with your hands. Next, sprinkle with the fresh ginger and rub that in as well. Season the chicken with salt and pepper, then pour the onion, garlic, and oil from the saucepan over it. Place a slice of butter on top of each one.

3. Bake the chicken for about 35 minutes, basting it with the juices about halfway through. When the chicken is cooked (it will look opaque when pierced deeply in the thickest part), transfer it to a warmed serving plate. Then place the pan over medium heat. Add the wine and chopped stem ginger, stir, and let it boil and reduce into a syrupy sauce. Then, off heat, stir in the yogurt. Pour the sauce over the chicken and sprinkle with the scallions.

Winter

Braised Chicken with 30 Cloves of Garlic
Serves 4

1 (4-pound) chicken

Salt and freshly ground black pepper to taste

1 tablespoon butter

1 tablespoon olive oil

30 garlic cloves, unpeeled (from 3 to 4 heads)

6 small sprigs fresh rosemary, plus 1 tablespoon rosemary leaves, bruised and chopped

1¼ cups dry white wine

For the sealing paste

1⅔ cup all-purpose flour, plus a little extra for dusting

You will also need a flameproof casserole large enough to hold the chicken comfortably, preferably oval, about 5 quarts.

Gently simmered, the garlic here mellows beautifully, losing much of its pungency and turning into golden sweet nuggets that are served like a vegetable alongside the juicy chicken. Because the whole bird along with the garlic, white wine, and seasonings are sealed inside the casserole with a flour paste, the chicken steams as it roasts, resulting in perfectly cooked meat and delectable pan juices that are all you need for sauce.

1. First of all, preheat the oven to 400°F. Dry the chicken as much as possible with paper towels and season it well. Next, melt the butter and oil in the casserole, then, keeping the heat fairly high, brown the chicken carefully on all sides. This will seem a bit awkward, but all you do is protect your hands with a cloth and hold the chicken by its legs, turning it into different positions until it is a good golden color all over; this will take 10 to 15 minutes in all. After that, remove the chicken from the casserole. Add the garlic and rosemary sprigs, toss these around, then replace the chicken, and sprinkle the chopped rosemary all over the chicken. Next, pour the wine all around it and let it gently come up to a simmer.

2. Meanwhile, place the flour in a bowl and stir in about ⅔ cup cold water to make a soft but not sticky dough. Divide the dough into 4 pieces and roll each one into a cylinder about 9 inches long on a lightly floured surface. Now position these all around the rim of the casserole, overlapping if needed – it doesn't matter what they look like. Place the casserole lid carefully on top, pressing down gently and making sure there are no gaps. Alternatively, simply place a double sheet of aluminum foil over the casserole before putting the lid on.

3. Now place the casserole in the oven and cook for 1¼ hours. Remove the lid and let the chicken continue to roast for another 10 minutes to crisp the skin. Next, transfer the chicken to a platter and let it rest for 10 minutes before carving. Serve the carved chicken with the garlic cloves alongside and the cooking juices poured around it. The idea is to squash the garlic cloves with a knife to release all the creamy pulp and, as you eat, dip the pieces of chicken into it.

Honey-Ginger Marinated Chicken Breasts with Mango Salsa
Serves 4

4 boneless chicken breasts, preferably with skin on (about 6 oz each)

For the marinade

2 tablespoons honey

1 (1-inch) piece of fresh ginger, peeled and finely grated

1 teaspoon ground ginger

2 garlic cloves, crushed

Zest and juice of ½ lime

Salt and freshly ground black pepper to taste

For the salsa

⅓ cup golden raisins

Zest and juice of 1 lime

1 ripe medium mango

½ red bell pepper, deseeded and chopped

½ medium red onion, finely chopped

1 green hot chili, deseeded and finely chopped

¼ cup fresh cilantro leaves, for garnish

You will also need a shallow ceramic, enameled cast-iron, or tempered glass ovenproof dish just large enough to hold the chicken breasts comfortably.

This is a quick and easy recipe that's helpful for busy people because it needs to be prepared ahead, preferably the day before. Serve it with potatoes that have been brushed with saffron oil after par-boiling, before being roasted at the same temperature as the chicken for 40-50 minutes or until really crunchy. For the saffron oil, mix a generous pinch of saffron stamens with a tablespoon of olive oil.

1. Begin this by marinating the chicken. Make 2 long cuts in each chicken breast, about ¼ inch deep, then place the chicken breasts neatly in the dish. Now whisk all of the marinade ingredients in a bowl, then pour this over the chicken breasts, turning them around in the marinade to get them well coated. You now need to cover the dish with plastic wrap and refrigerate overnight. Next, for the salsa, place the raisins with the lime zest and juice in a small bowl so they can plump up overnight. Cover them with plastic wrap and refrigerate.

2. When you are ready to cook the chicken, preheat the oven to 425°F. Then remove the plastic wrap from the chicken and baste each breast with the marinade. Bake on a high oven rack (or the next one down if you are roasting potatoes at the same time) for 20 to 30 minutes, until the chicken feels firm when pressed in the center.

3. While the chicken is cooking, finish the salsa. Remove the skin from the mango, using a potato peeler or sharp knife. Then slice all the flesh away from the stone and chop it into small pieces – about ¼-inch dice. Then add it to the raisins, along with the remaining salsa ingredients, and garnish, just before serving, with the cilantro leaves.

4. Serve the cooked chicken with some of the salsa spooned over and the rest served separately, along with a bowl of roasted potatoes, which have been sprinkled with a little salt.

Chicken Stir-Fry with Broccoli, Fresh Shiitakes, and Cashews
Serves 4

4 skinless and boneless chicken breasts (about 1 ¼ pounds total)

3 tablespoons cornstarch

¾ teaspoon five-spice powder

6 tablespoons Japanese soy sauce

6 ounces shiitake mushrooms

2 cups broccoli florets

4 scallions

3 tablespoons peanut or other flavorless oil

1 cup (4 oz) raw cashew nuts

1 medium onion, finely chopped

3 cloves garlic, crushed

1 tablespoons fresh ginger, peeled and grated

1 teaspoon salt

⅓ cup rice wine or dry sherry, mixed with 3 tablespoons Japanese soy sauce

You will also need a wok or a very large skillet with a lid.

Speed is the great thing about a stir-fry. Once you have all your ingredients prepared, the actual cooking time is less than 10 minutes. Chinese five-spice powder imparts a heady, authentic flavor to this dish, but if you can't find it in your market, substitute ¼ teaspoon ground cinnamon mixed with ⅛ teaspoon each allspice and black pepper, and a pinch of ground cloves.

1. First, you need to cut the chicken into strips, which should be about ¼ inch x 2 inches. Then place them in a large bowl and toss with the cornstarch and five-spice powder so that all the strips get an even coating. Next, add 3 tablespoons soy sauce and give the whole thing a really good toss. Then cover the bowl and leave it aside for 30 minutes while you prepare all the other ingredients.

2. Now stem the shiitakes and cut the caps into thin slices. Cut the broccoli stalks into very thin diagonal slices and slice the tops. What you do with the scallions is chop the white part quite small and the green part into very thin shreds.

3. When you are ready to cook the stir-fry, first heat 1 tablespoon of the oil in the wok over high heat. When it's very hot, fry the cashews for 45 to 60 seconds until they are a lovely golden brown color. Keep them on the move all the time, then transfer to a plate with a slotted spoon. Now add another tablespoon of oil and, again, when it becomes really hot, keep the heat high and stir-fry the chicken in two batches, giving each batch 2 to 3 minutes, until it turns crisp and golden and becomes cooked through. As the chicken cooks, transfer it to a plate and keep warm.

4. Now add the last tablespoon of oil, this time keeping the heat at medium. Stir-fry the chopped onion, garlic, and ginger for about 2 minutes. Then turn the heat up to high again, add the mushrooms and broccoli and stir-fry these for another minute, tossing them around all the time so they come in contact with the heat on all sides. Return the chicken and cashews to the wok and season with the salt. Mix the rice wine with the remaining 3 tablespoons soy sauce and stir it into the wok. Turn the heat down to medium, then add the chopped whites of the scallions, cover, and let it all cook for just 1 minute. Serve immediately on a bed of rice noodles or plain steamed rice, with the reserved scallion greens sprinkled over.

Fried Chicken Breasts Stuffed with Cheddar and Chives
Serves 4

4 skinless and boneless chicken breasts (about 6 oz each)

4 ounces sharp Cheddar cheese

1 tablespoon finely chopped chives

¼ cup all-purpose flour

Salt and freshly ground black pepper to taste

2 large eggs, beaten

1 cup fresh white breadcrumbs (make them in a blender or food processor from day-old bread)

2 to 3 tablespoons peanut or other flavorless oil

You could think of this as an Americanized version of chicken Kiev. Instead of being stuffed with flavored butter, though, the skinless, boneless breasts are filled with Cheddar cheese and chives before being coated with breadcrumbs and pan-fried. Use a good-quality cheese here; the more aged, the sharper it will be, so choose according to your taste. Serve with a watercress salad.

1. First of all, take each of the chicken breasts and using a small, very sharp knife, make a cut to form a pocket in each one lengthways. Then shred the cheese and mix it with the chives and fill each of the pockets with a quarter of the cheese mixture.

2. Next, in a shallow dish, season the flour with salt and pepper. Roll the chicken breasts in the seasoned flour and shake off the excess. Beat the eggs in a shallow dish, and place the breadcrumbs in another dish. Coat the breasts with beaten egg and then roll each one in breadcrumbs, pressing the breadcrumbs firmly all round to get an even coating.

3. Now heat 2 tablespoons of the oil in a large skillet and, keeping the heat at medium, cook the chicken breasts for 10 minutes on each side, by which time they will be golden brown and cooked through, adding a little more oil, if necessary. Drain them briefly on paper towels and sprinkle with salt and freshly ground black pepper before serving.

Coq au Vin
Serves 4-6

2 tablespoons butter

1 tablespoon peanut or other flavorless oil

1 (5-pound) chicken, cut into 8 serving pieces

8 ounces slab bacon, rind discarded, cut into thick strips, or cubed pancetta

16 shallots or button onions, peeled

2 garlic cloves, crushed

2 sprigs fresh thyme

Salt and freshly ground black pepper to taste

2 bay leaves

1 (750-ml) bottle hearty red wine

8 ounces cremini mushrooms

1½ tablespoons softened butter and 1 tablespoon all-purpose flour, mashed into a paste

Chopped fresh parsley, for garnish (optional)

You will also need a medium casserole, wide and shallow enough to hold the chicken pieces in one layer.

Classic sautéed chicken braised in red wine with bacon and mushrooms is a hearty dish, equally as appropriate for company as for a special family meal. Serve with buttered noodles or creamy mashed potatoes and sugar snap peas.

1. Melt the butter with the oil in a large skillet. Add the chicken pieces, skin side down, and cook until they are nicely golden, then turn them and color the other side. You will have to do this in three or four batches – don't overcrowd the pan. As they are ready, transfer the chicken from the skillet with a slotted spoon to the casserole. The casserole should be large enough for the chicken pieces to be arranged in one layer yet deep enough so that they can be completely covered with liquid later.

2. Now brown the bacon also in the skillet and add them to the chicken. Finally, brown the shallots a little in the bacon fat and add them too. Next, place the garlic and the thyme among the chicken pieces, season with freshly ground pepper and just a little salt, and add a couple of bay leaves. Pour in the wine and put a lid on the pot. Simmer gently for 45 minutes to 1 hour, or until the chicken is tender. During the last 15 minutes of the cooking, add the mushrooms and stir them into the liquid.

3. Using a slotted spoon, transfer the chicken, bacon, onions, and mushrooms to a warmed serving dish and keep warm. Discard the bay leaves and thyme at this stage. Now bring the liquid to a fast boil over high heat and reduce it by about one-third. Next, whisk in the butter and flour paste. Bring it to a boil, whisking all the time, until the sauce has thickened. Pour the sauce over the chicken. If you like, sprinkle some chopped parsley over the chicken and make it look pretty.

Baked Chicken with Fragrant Indian Spices
Serves 4

1 (4-pound) chicken, cut into 8 pieces

1 tablespoon grated fresh ginger or 1 ½ teaspoons ground ginger

2 garlic cloves, crushed

2 teaspoons ground turmeric

1 ½ tablespoons peanut or other flavorless oil

Salt and freshly ground black pepper to taste

For the spice sauce

1 teaspoon whole coriander seeds

¾ teaspoon whole cumin seeds

8 whole cardamom pods

2 tablespoons butter

1 ½ teaspoons peanut or other flavorless oil

2 onions, very finely chopped

1 medium green pepper, deseeded and finely chopped

2 dried red chilies, deseeded and very finely chopped

1 bay leaf, crumbled

⅔ cup plain low-fat yogurt, mixed with ¼ cup hot water

Salt to taste

You will also need an oblong roasting pan or ovenproof dish large enough to hold the chicken pieces in a single layer.

To magnify flavor, the chicken here is lightly marinated prior to being baked, so be sure to allow at least an hour or two before cooking. The spiced yogurt sauce can be prepared while the chicken is marinating or after you put it in the oven. Serve with rice tossed with raisins and cashews and mango chutney.

1. About 2 hours before cooking, arrange the chicken in the roasting pan. In a small bowl, mix together the ginger, garlic, and turmeric with the oil. Now, with a sharp knife, make several incisions in the chicken pieces. Season the chicken with salt and pepper, then coat them as evenly as possible with the spice mixture. Leave in a cool place (but not in the refrigerator) so that the flavors penetrate for about an hour.

2. When you're ready to cook the chicken, preheat the oven to 400°F. Place the pan dish on the highest oven rack. Cook, uncovered, about 20 minutes or until the chicken pieces are a nice golden color.

3. Meanwhile, prepare the whole spices. First of all, toast the coriander, cumin, and cardamom in a heavy-bottomed skillet over medium heat for about 1 minute until they turn one shade darker, tossing them to keep them on the move. This warming of the spices helps to draw out all the flavor. Discard the cardamom pods but make sure you keep all the seeds from inside. Now grind and crush the seeds finely, either with mortar and pestle or in a spice grinder.

4. Next, melt the butter and oil together in a skillet. Add the onions and green pepper, and cook for 5 minutes. Now add the crushed spices, chilies, and crumbled bay leaf, stir, and cook for another 5 minutes. Remove the pan from heat, stir in the yogurt mixture, and add a little salt. Pour the spice sauce all over the chicken pieces. Cover the pan with a double sheet of aluminum foil. Bake for 30 minutes longer with the heat reduced to 350°F. Remove the foil and let it cook for another 10 minutes until the chicken shows no sign of pink when pierced at the tip of a knife.

Chicken Satays with Spicy Peanut Sauce
Serves 6 as a starter or 4 as a main course

4 skinless and boneless chicken breasts (about 6 oz each)

For the marinade

1 tablespoon honey

1 tablespoon Japanese soy sauce

A few drops of hot red pepper sauce

1 garlic clove, crushed through a press

1 teaspoon grated fresh ginger

For the sauce

1½ tablespoons peanut or other
flavorless oil

3 shallots, finely chopped

1½ to 2 red chilies, deseeded and chopped

1 teaspoon grated fresh ginger

2 garlic cloves, crushed under a knife

1 cup roasted peanuts

2 tablespoons fresh lime juice

1½ tablespoons Japanese soy sauce

1 tablespoon packed light brown sugar

1 tablespoon cilantro leaves

You will also need about 40 (8-inch) bamboo skewers.

Everyone loves sweet-spicy peanut sauce, and this excellent version is whipped up in a flash in a food processor. The satays can be served as a hot appetizer or as a first course, accompanied with a little cucumber salad, if you like.

1. First of all, prepare the marinade, which simply means putting all the ingredients in a bowl and whisking them thoroughly together. Then, to prepare the chicken, take each chicken breast and pull off the tender, and cut the tender in half lengthways. Next, slice the main breast in half horizontally to make 2 thinner, flat slices. Then cut each of these into 3 or 4 strips lengthways: you should get about 8 or 9 strips from each chicken breast. Put the strips into the marinade, tossing and stirring them well until they get a good coating. Next, cover the bowl and leave it aside in a cool place for at least 30 minutes – although 2 hours would be better.

2. To prepare the sauce, first heat the peanut oil in a skillet pan and, over medium heat, soften the shallots for about 3 minutes. Then add the chilies, ginger, and garlic and cook them for another 1½ minutes. Next, add the peanuts and stir them for about 1½ minutes. After that, remove the pan from the heat and allow everything to cool. As soon as it's cool, scrape everything into a food processor with lime juice, soy sauce, brown sugar, cilantro, and 3 tablespoons of water and process until roughly chopped. Do be careful not to overprocess, as the sauce needs to have some texture. After that, transfer it to a serving bowl.

3. All the above can be done well in advance, but before you cook the satays, if you are using the bamboo skewers, don't forget to soak them in hot water for about 30 minutes to prevent them from burning. Then, when you're ready to cook the chicken, preheat the broiler on high for 10 minutes.

4. Meanwhile, thread the strips of chicken on to each skewer, threading them in a loose "S" shape (see right). Then broil them about 3 inches from the heat source, giving them 3 to 4 minutes on each side. Serve on warm plates with the peanut sauce passed separately.

Braised Chicken with Bacon, Mushrooms, and Root Vegetables
Serves 4

3 tablespoons olive oil

8 ounces slab bacon, rind discarded, cut into thick strips, or chopped pancetta

12 shallots or boiling onions, peeled

One (3-pound) chicken

4 medium carrots, peeled and cut into 1 inch chunks or 6 whole baby carrots, peeled and trimmed

4 small turnips, peeled and quartered

1 garlic clove, crushed

2 cups chicken stock, such as Chicken Giblet Stock (see page 127)

1¼ cups dry white wine

6 sprigs of parsley

2 sprigs of fresh thyme

A few celery leaves (if you happen to have them)

1 bay leaf

Salt and freshly ground black pepper to taste

8 ounces cremini mushrooms, sliced

1½ tablespoons softened butter and 1 tablespoon all-purpose flour mashed into a paste

You will also need a flameproof casserole large enough to hold the chicken comfortably, about 5 quarts.

In flavor, this is a lot like a stew, but because you lift a whole chicken out of the pot to carve, it makes for a more dramatic presentation. Serve with a potato gratin and peas.

1. First, heat 1 tablespoon of the oil in the casserole, then cook the bacon a little with the shallots. When they have colored a bit, remove them with a slotted spoon to a plate and keep them on one side.

2. Now, add the remaining 2 tablespoons of oil and when it is fairly hot, fry the chicken whole. This will seem a bit awkward, but all you do is protect your hands with a cloth and hold the chicken by its legs, turning it into different positions until it is a good golden color all over; this will take 10 to 15 minutes in all. Then remove it from the casserole. Next, add the carrots, turnips, and garlic to the pot and cook for about 5 minutes, stirring them all around so that they brown slightly. Now put the bacon and onions back in the pan. Push everything to the sides and sit the chicken in the center. Next, pour in the stock and wine, add the parsley and thyme, tied into a bundle (if using the celery leaves, tie them with the other herbs), and bay leaf and season with salt and pepper. Bring to a simmering point, then transfer the casserole to the oven (the casserole should be without a lid, but place a piece of foil over the chicken breast) and let it cook for 30 minutes, uncovering and basting the chicken breast now and then with the surrounding stock. After 30 minutes, remove the foil, add the sliced mushrooms, then bake for another 30 minutes, again basting fairly often with the juices. When the chicken is cooked, take the casserole from the oven, remove the chicken, drain it well, and put it on a warmed serving dish. Surround it with the well-drained vegetables and bacon, and discard the bay leaf and herbs.

3. Now place the casserole over a direct heat and boil the liquid fiercely to reduce it by about a third. Then whisk in the butter and flour paste, and bring back to a boil, whisking continuously until the sauce thickens. Taste to check the seasoning, then carve and serve the chicken and vegetables with the sauce poured over them.

Moroccan Chicken with Olives, Chickpeas, and Rice
Serves 4

¾ cup dried chickpeas (garbanzo beans)

1 tablespoon coriander seeds

1 teaspoon cumin seeds

½ teaspoon saffron threads

2 small, thin-skinned lemons

1 (3½- to 4-pound) chicken, cut into 8 pieces, or a mixture of 8 drumsticks and thighs

Salt and freshly ground black pepper to taste

2 large yellow peppers

2 large onions

2 tablespoons olive oil

16 large sprigs of cilantro

1 cup brown basmati rice

3 garlic cloves, chopped

2 fresh chilis, halved, deseeded, and finely chopped

1¼ cups chicken stock, such as Chicken Giblet Stock (see page 127)

¾ cup dry white wine

⅓ cup pitted black olives

⅓ cup pitted green olives

You will also need a wide, shallow, flameproof casserole, about 9 inches in diameter.

Chock full of black and green olives and flavored with lemon, cilantro, and fragrant spices, this makes a great one-dish meal. If you have an appropriately attractive pot, it can go right from the stove to the table.

1. There are two ways to deal with chickpeas. The easiest is to pop them into a bowl, cover them with cold water, and leave them overnight or for a minimum of 8 hours. But, if it slips your mind, what you can do is place them in a saucepan, cover them with cold water, and bring them up to a boil for 10 minutes. Then turn off the heat and let them soak for 3 hours. Either way, when you want to start making this recipe, the chickpeas need to be simmered for 20 minutes or until tender.

2. While they're simmering, preheat the oven to 350°F. Place a small skillet over medium heat, add the coriander seeds and cumin and stir them around in the hot pan for about 2 to 3 minutes or until they start to "dance" and change color. Then remove the seeds to a pestle and mortar, crush them coarsely, and transfer to a plate. Next, crush the saffron to a powder with the pestle and mortar, then squeeze out the juice of one of the lemons and add it to the saffron, stirring well.

3. Now prepare the chicken by seasoning the pieces with salt and pepper. Slice the peppers in half, remove the seeds and pith, and cut each half into four large pieces. The onions should be sliced roughly the same size as the peppers. Now heat 1 tablespoon of the olive oil in the casserole and, when it's really hot, brown the chicken pieces on all sides – don't overcrowd the pan; it's best to do it in two batches, four pieces at a time. After that, transfer the chicken pieces to a plate. Then add the remaining tablespoon of oil and turn the heat to its highest setting. When the oil is really hot, add the peppers and onions and cook them in the hot oil, moving them around until their edges are slightly blackened – this should take about 5 minutes – then turn the heat down. Strip the cilantro leaves from the stalks, wrap the leaves in a piece of plastic wrap, and refrigerate them. Then chop the cilantro stalks finely and add these to the peppers and onions, along with the rice, soaked chickpeas, garlic, chilies, and crushed spices. Then give everything a good stir to distribute all the ingredients.

4. Season well with salt and pepper, then combine the lemon and saffron mixture with the stock and wine, pour it into the casserole, and stir well. Cut the remaining lemon into thin slices and push these well into the liquid. Now scatter in the olives, and finally, place the chicken on top of everything. Cover tightly with the lid. Bake for 1 hour or until the rice is tender and the chicken is cooked through. Then, just before serving, scatter the reserved cilantro leaves on top and serve immediately on warmed serving plates.

Chicken Jambalaya
Serves 4-6

4 ounces smoked andouille, chorizo sausage, or hot kielbasa, peeled and cut into ¾-inch pieces

1 or 2 tablespoons olive oil

2 skinless and boneless chicken thighs (about 9 ounces total), cut into bite-sized pieces

1 medium onion, cut into ½-inch slices

2 celery ribs, trimmed and sliced on the diagonal into ½-inch pieces

1 yellow bell pepper, deseeded and cut into ½-inch slices

1 green chili, deseeded and finely chopped

2 garlic cloves, crushed

1 cup white long-grain rice

1 teaspoon hot red pepper sauce

2 cups hot chicken stock

3 medium tomatoes, dropped into boiling water for 1 minute, then peeled and chopped

1 bay leaf

Salt and freshly ground black pepper to taste

For the garnish

1 tablespoon roughly chopped fresh flat-leaf parsley

2 scallions, white and green parts, trimmed and finely sliced

You will also need a 10-inch skillet with a lid.

Cajun andouille would be the authentic sausage to use here, but since it is relatively hard to find outside of Louisiana, you can use chorizo or hot kielbasa. You could also substitute chunks of flavorful smoked ham for half the sausage and add some shrimp for the final 5 minutes of cooking.

1. First of all, heat the skillet over high heat and brown the chorizo, without adding any fat, then transfer them to a plate and set aside. Then add a tablespoon of the oil and, when it's hot, brown the chicken and transfer to the plate with the sausage. Next, add and cook the onions for 2 to 3 minutes to brown them a little at the edges, then return the sausage and chicken to the pan and add the celery, yellow pepper, chili, and garlic. Continue to cook for 4 or 5 minutes, until the celery and pepper are also softened and lightly tinged brown at the edges, adding a little more oil if you need to.

2. Now stir in the rice to get a good coating of oil. Add the hot sauce to the hot chicken stock. Next, add the chopped tomatoes and bay leaf to the pan, then pour in the stock and bring to a simmer. Season with salt and freshly ground black pepper, give it all one stir, and push the rice down into the liquid. Now turn the heat to low, put a lid on, and let it barely simmer for 20 minutes. Then, check that the rice is tender and add a little more stock, if necessary. Remove from the heat and let stand, covered, for 5 minutes. Serve, garnished with the chopped parsley and scallions.

Chicken Pot Pie with Carrots and Leeks
Serves 4

2 ½ cups hard cider or 1 ¾ cups dry white wine and ½ cup apple juice

4 medium carrots, peeled and cut into ⅛-inch slices

1 sprig of fresh thyme

1 bay leaf

Salt and freshly ground black pepper to taste

4 medium leeks

4 boneless chicken breasts, preferably with the skin on (about 6 oz each)

One sheet (½ of a 17.3-oz package) frozen puff pastry, thawed

All-purpose flour, for rolling out the pastry

1 large egg, lightly beaten

1 tablespoon finely grated Parmesan, for sprinkling

For the sauce

2 ½ cups milk

3 tablespoons all-purpose flour

3 tablespoons butter

A pinch of cayenne pepper

½ cup shredded sharp Cheddar

¼ cup freshly grated Parmesan

Salt and freshly ground black pepper to taste

A little freshly grated nutmeg

You will also need a round oven-proof casserole or soufflé dish with a capacity of about 2 quarts and a diameter of about 9 inches.

Nothing is more comforting on a gray winter day than a steaming hot chicken pot pie. A nice surprise here is the combination of cheddar and parmesan cheeses added to the cream sauce base. You can vary the vegetables by replacing half the leeks with mushrooms.

1. First, pour the cider into a medium saucepan, along with the carrots, thyme, bay leaf, and some salt and pepper. Bring to a simmering point, then cover with a lid, and simmer gently for 5 minutes. Now cut off the tough green tops from the leeks, then make a vertical split halfway down the center of each leek and run them under cold water to wash away any hidden grit. Then slice them in half lengthways and chop into ½-inch slices. Add the chicken and leeks to the pan and simmer covered for another 10 minutes.

2. For the sauce, all you do is place the milk, flour, butter, and cayenne pepper into a medium saucepan and place it over a gentle heat. Then, using a balloon whisk, begin to whisk while bringing it to a gentle simmer. Whisk continually until you have a smooth, glossy sauce, and simmer very gently for 5 minutes. Then add the cheeses and whisk again, allowing them to melt. Then season with salt, freshly ground black pepper, and some freshly grated nutmeg. Next, drain the chicken and vegetables, reserving the liquid, but not the bay leaf and thyme. Now pour the liquid back into the pan, bring it to a boil, and reduce to about ¼ cup. Meanwhile, skin the chicken and cut the flesh into bite-sized strips.

3. Preheat the oven to 400°F. Now stir the cheese sauce into the reduced cooking liquid and bring to a simmer. Stir in the chicken, carrots, and leeks, then transfer to the dish.

4. Next, to make a lid, roll out the pastry until about ⅛ inch thick on a lightly floured surface. Cut out a 9-inch round. Cut a ½ inch–wide strip from the trimmings. Now dampen the edge of the dish with water and press the strip of pastry around the rim. Dampen the strip and carefully lift the pastry round over the top. Press it firmly over the edge to get a good seal all around, then trim away excess pastry with a knife. Cut out leaf shapes from the remaining pastry trimmings. Brush the surface of the pie with some beaten egg, and arrange the leaves on top. Now, brush the leaves with beaten egg, sprinkle with Parmesan, and bake on the baking sheet for 20 minutes, or until the pastry is golden brown.

Holiday Roast Chicken with Sausage, Apple, and Sage Stuffing
Serves 6-8

For the apple, sage, and onion stuffing

3 slices fresh white bread, crusts removed

1 Golden Delicious apple, peeled, cored and quartered

1 small onion, quartered

1 ½ tablespoons tablespoon fresh sage leaves

1 tablespoon fresh parsley leaves

Reserved chicken livers from the giblets (use the rest of the giblets to make the stock for the gravy)

8 ounces ground pork or bulk sausage

¼ teaspoon powdered mace

Salt and freshly ground black pepper to taste

For the roast chicken

One (5- to 6-pound) chicken

4 tablespoons butter, at room temperature

Salt and freshly ground black pepper to taste

8 slices bacon

You will also need a large, flameproof roasting pan.

This is a family roast chicken, moist and succulent for Sunday lunch, with lots of crispy bacon and some very savoury stuffing. Serve with Traditional Chicken Giblet Gravy (you will need to make the stock ahead of time, see page 127), Traditional Bread Sauce, and Balsamic-Sage Cranberry Sauce (see page 128).

1. If you have a food processor, making stuffing is simple: all you do is switch the motor on, add the bread, and process to crumbs, then add the apple, onion, sage, and parsley, and process till everything is finely chopped. Next, trim any sinewy bits from the chicken livers, rinse the livers under cold water, pat them dry, then add them to the processor, together with the pork, mace, salt, and pepper. Give a few pulses in the processor until it is all thoroughly blended, remove the stuffing from the processor with a spatula, then place in a plastic bag and refrigerate until needed. If you're doing this by hand, just finely chop all the ingredients, combine in a bowl, and refrigerate as above.

2. For the chicken, preheat the oven to 375°F. First of all, the chicken needs to be stuffed, and to do this, you begin at the neck end, where you'll find a flap of loose skin: gently loosen this away from the breast and you'll be able to make a triangular pocket. Loosely pack the stuffing inside, making a neat round shape on the outside, then tuck the neck flap under the bird's back and secure it with a small skewer or toothpick. Place the remaining stuffing in the body cavity (the fat in the pork will melt and help to keep the bird moist inside). Now place the chicken on a rack in the roasting pan and smear the butter over the chicken, using your hands, and making sure you don't leave any part of the surface unbuttered.

3. Season the chicken all over with salt and pepper, then arrange 7 bacon slices, slightly overlapping, in a row along the breast. Cut the last slice in half and place one piece on each leg. Then place the chicken in the oven on the center rack and cook for 20 minutes per pound, plus 10 to 20 minutes extra – this will be 1 hour 50 minutes to 2 hours for a 5-pound bird, or 2 hours 10 minutes to 2 hours 20 minutes for a 6-pound bird. The chicken is cooked if the juices run clear when the thickest part of the leg is pierced with a skewer. It is important to baste the chicken at least three times during the

cooking – spooning over the juices mingling with the bacon fat and butter helps to keep the flesh succulent.

4. During the last basting (about half an hour before the chicken is cooked), remove the now crisp bacon slices and keep them warm. If they are not crisp, just put them around the chicken to finish off. For the final 15 minutes of cooking, hike the heat up to 425°F (220°C), which will give the skin that final golden crispiness.

5. When the chicken is cooked it is important to leave it in the warm kitchen (near the oven), covered in aluminum foil for 30 minutes, to allow it to "relax." This is because when the chicken is cooking all the juices bubble up to the surface (if you look inside the oven you will actually see this happening just under the skin), and the "relaxing" allows time for all these precious juices to seep back into the flesh. It also makes it much easier to carve. When you serve the chicken, make sure everyone gets some crispy bacon and stuffing.

Traditional Gravy and Other Sauces

Traditional Chicken Giblet Gravy

Makes about 2 cups to serve 6 to 8 people

This is a real chicken-flavored gravy to serve with a family roast chicken for Sunday lunch. Serve with the recipe for Traditional Roast Chicken with Apple, Sage, and Onion Stuffing on page 124. You should make the stock ahead of time to allow it to cool completely before you need to use it.

For the chicken giblet stock

8 ounces chicken giblets from 1 or 2 large chickens (when not cooking chicken giblets, freeze them to use in this recipe)

1 medium carrot, roughly chopped

½ onion

A few fresh parsley stalks

A sprig of fresh thyme

1 bay leaf

½ teaspoon whole black peppercorns

Salt to taste

For the gravy

The juices left in the roasting pan from cooking a roast chicken

3 tablespoons all-purpose flour

3 cups chicken giblet stock (but the exact amount will depend on how thick you like your gravy)

Salt and freshly ground black pepper to taste

1. For the stock, begin by simply placing the giblets, 3½ cups water, carrot, onion, herbs, peppercorns, and a little salt in a medium saucepan and simmer very gently with the lid almost on for 2 hours. Now strain the stock into a bowl. Cool, then chill in the refrigerator. Any fat on the surface is easily removed when cold.

2. To make the gravy, after removing the chicken from the roasting pan in which it has cooked, tilt the pan and skim off most of the clear fat, which you will see separates quite clearly from the juices – you need to leave about 2 tablespoons of fat behind in the pan.

3. Now place the roasting pan over fairly low heat, and when the juices begin to sizzle, sprinkle in the flour, stirring vigorously with a wooden spoon until you get a smooth paste. Then whisk in the giblet stock, little by little.

4. Whisk the gravy thoroughly until all the stock is incorporated. Now bring it up to a simmer, season with salt and freshly ground black pepper. Then pour the piping hot gravy into a warm sauceboat and pass separately with the roast chicken.

English Bread Sauce
Serves 8

Traditional bread sauce is one of the great, classic British sauces, but it has suffered either from not being made properly or – worst of all – being made from a mix or packet. The real thing is beautifully creamy and the perfect accompaniment to chicken. Leave the milk to infuse for two hours or more before making the sauce.

1 large onion

15 to 18 whole cloves or freshly grated nutmeg

1 bay leaf

8 black peppercorns

2 cups whole milk

1 cup freshly made breadcrumbs from a 2-day old white loaf with crusts removed

4 tablespoons butter

2 tablespoons heavy cream

Salt and freshly ground black pepper to taste

1. Cut the onion in half and stick the cloves in it (how many you use is a personal matter – I happen to like a pronounced clove flavor). If you don't like them at all, you can add some freshly grated nutmeg to the milk instead. Place the onion – studded with cloves – plus the bay leaf and the peppercorns, in a medium saucepan together with the milk. Add some salt, then bring everything just to a boil. Take off the heat, cover the pan, and leave in a warm place for the milk to infuse for

2 hours or more. When you're ready to make the sauce, remove the onion, bay leaf, and peppercorns and keep them on one side. Stir the breadcrumbs into the milk and add 2 tablespoons of butter. Cook over very low heat, stirring now and then, until the crumbs have swollen and thickened the sauce – about 15 minutes.

2. If you are not serving right away, replace the clove-studded onion and leave the pan in a warm place until the sauce is needed. Just before serving, remove the onion. Reheat gently, then beat in the remaining 2 tablespoons butter and the cream and taste to check the seasoning. Pour into a warm sauceboat and serve hot.

Balsamic-Sage Cranberry Sauce
Serves 6-8

Serve this with traditional roast chicken.

¾ cup (1 8-oz can) cranberry sauce

3 tablespoons fresh sage

3 tablespoons balsamic vinegar

Salt and freshly ground black pepper to taste

All you do here is combine everything in a small saucepan and whisk over a gentle heat until the cranberry sauce has melted. Then pour the sauce into a serving bowl and let stand until needed (it doesn't need reheating – it's served at room temperature).

How to Carve a Chicken

When a chicken is cooked, the heat in the oven causes all the internal juices to bubble up to the surface just under the skin – sometimes you can see the skin almost flapping with the amount of juice inside it. Because of this you should always allow the bird to rest for at least 15 minutes before carving it, so that all the wonderful juices travel back from where they came and keep everything lovely and moist. The fibers of the chicken will also relax, and this will make carving easier.

Carving is very easy, provided you have a sharp knife and follow the instructions given below. A lot of people imagine they can't carve very well, but the truth is probably that the knife they are using simply isn't sharp enough. What you really need to do is buy a good-quality carving knife and a sharpening steel and simply practice. I was taught by a butcher, who said knives should be sharpened a little and often. I have also found the following advice good for anyone who wants to learn: hold the steel horizontally in front of you and the knife vertically, then slide the blade of the knife down, allowing the tip to touch the steel, first on one side of the steel and then on the other. If you really can't face it, there are knife sharpeners available.

Insert the knife between the leg and body and remove the thigh and drumstick in one piece (see opposite, top right).

Remove the wing on the same side, then slice the breast (see bottom left).

Repeat this on the other side of the bird. Finally, divide the drumstick and thigh, cutting through the joint so you have two leg portions (see bottom right).

Index

Picture credits

Delia Smith is an international culinary phenomenon, whose best-selling cookbooks have sold over 17 million copies.

Delia's other books include *How To Cook Books One*, *Two* and *Three*, her *Vegetarian Collection*, the *Complete Illustrated Cookery Course*, *One Is Fun*, the *Summer* and *Winter Collections*, and *Christmas*. Delia is the creator of Canary Catering and now runs five successful restaurants and a series of regular food and wine workshops.

She is married to the writer and editor Michael Wynn Jones and they live in England.

Visit Delia's website at www.deliaonline.com